Blye, Private Eye

BLYE, PRIVATE EYE

Nicholas Pileggi

P❦P
A Playboy Press Book

Mr. Blye's case histories are true, but the names, places, and certain investigative techniques have been altered to protect the privacy of the subjects involved.

Library of Congress Cataloging in Publication Data

Pileggi, Nicholas.
    Blye, private eye.

       1. Blye, Irwin. 2. Detectives—United States.
I. Title.
HV8083.B59P55   363.2'092'4 [B]   76-55344
ISBN 0-87223-475-4

SPADE: Got 'em?

COP: Got 'em.

SPADE: Swell! Here's another one for yuh. She killed Miles. Oh, and I've got some exhibits: the boy's gun, one of Cairo's, a thousand dollar bill I was supposed to be bribed with. And this black statuette here that all the fuss was about.

COP: It's heavy. What is it?

SPADE: The, er, stuff that dreams are made of.

COP: Huh?

The Maltese Falcon by DASHIELL HAMMETT
(Screenplay by John Huston)

Blye, Private Eye

1 When Edna Moore heard the car door

open she knew she was in trouble. There was something about the sound. She had parked her own car in the municipal lot across the street from the Spartanburg, South Carolina, J.C. Penney's and she was squinting into the bright late morning sun as she approached the store.

J.C. Penney's is the centerpiece of Spartanburg's busiest shopping center. Crowds of shoppers moved around Edna that day, but an intuition told her that the men in the beat-up white sedan parked alongside the curb ahead meant trouble. She couldn't explain it; she was not even sure they had seen her. Nevertheless, her instincts caused her to quicken her pace as she walked past the car and on toward Penney's. That was when she heard the car door open and the engine start up. The roar of an old engine and a battered muffler seemed to cloak her in noise. It was all so quick. With the department store entrance just a few feet ahead and people walking only a whisper away, Edna Moore felt a presence beside her.

He was enormous—about six feet tall and weighing more than three hundred pounds. He blocked from view everything behind him. He grabbed her left arm with one huge hand and pressed a knife against her waist with the other. She looked down and saw a surprisingly small blade glistening in the sun.

"Get in the car," the fat man said. Before she could think what to answer he had swept her toward the open car door.

Within seconds Edna Moore found herself on the floor of the rear seat. The door closed with a slam. She heard the roar and could feel the vibration of the car's muffler as they sped away. Edna could not hear what the men were saying over the noise of the car. The fat man leaned over the seat talking and laughing with his two friends in the front while resting his feet on her back and on the seat of her slacks. Every once in a while he would press down hard. The worn carpeting and the brownish-gray upholstery were dusty and filled with grit. She was terrified and she felt dirty.

Edna Kay Moore was a nineteen-year-old student at nearby Davidson College. She was small, five feet four, pretty, and had a freshly scrubbed look. Her soft brown hair, shoulder length, bounced lightly off her shoulders when she walked. Her large brown eyes looked bright, if not very worldly. The big man had lifted her 110 pounds off the ground effortlessly and had thrown her onto the car's floorboards before she knew what had happened.

Edna had left her house in Gaffney, South Carolina, about ten o'clock that morning. She had driven straight to the airport in Spartanburg where she took a flying lesson at the Ore Aviation School. For approximately an hour, Edna and her instructor flew a dual-control trainer high above Spartanburg and Greenville. After her lesson she drove to the shopping center and parked her car in the municipal lot across the street. Edna disliked parking in the shopping center lot because it was always crowded and she didn't like having to walk past row after row of parked cars to reach Penney's. If it was not the smart guys waiting for their wives, it was their heirs in panel trucks who could not let a girl pass without a remark of some kind. She usually paid twenty-five cents for a spot in the municipal lot, but it was worth it.

She had lived near Spartanburg all her life and there were few roads she had not driven many times. She was certain that they had left Spartanburg on route 9, since the journey for the first hour was a stop-and-go affair. Had the men taken U.S. 85 out of Spartanburg they would have been able to drive nonstop on a seventy-mile-per-hour highway.

Edna surmised that they were driving through Pacolet Mills and Jonesville and Bonham. A variety of sounds of which she had never known she was aware helped her identify the road. When the car pulled into a parking area, Edna was almost certain that she was in Union, a town thirty miles south of Spartanburg. The driver left and returned in a few minutes. One of the other men said something and she heard him reply, "Yeah, I got." He went away again and she was left with the fat man in the rear seat and the second man in the front seat. That was when it started. The fat man began pinching her buttocks and tickling her waist. As she yelled and squirmed he managed to get his hands under her sweater and blouse. The man in the front laughed. Suddenly the fat man seemed to lose interest. Edna pleaded with them to let her go. She was due at work in a donut shop in Cowpona at one o'clock and if she didn't show up she would be missed. They laughed at this and went back to their conversation. The fat man continued to maul her at intervals, whenever there was a break in the conversation.

During her struggles, Edna managed to get a good look at the fat man. He was grotesque. Young, in his late twenties or early thirties, his head was a mass of curly and greasy sandy brown hair and he had a thick, curly beard. Rolls of fat covered his arms—which were thick with black hair—stomach, and neck and he sweated heavily. He had a round moon face, thick lips, a wheezing, almost asthmatic voice, and a ruddy complexion. He spoke in an ungrammatical backwoods dialect. A blue, short-sleeved shirt with dark half-mooned sweat stains under each arm covered his bulk.

The men were not talking very loudly, but Edna could catch bits about a beach somewhere and about having been surfing. The man in the front talked about a film he had recently seen in which a woman was eaten by a shark. Both men seemed to be amused by the scene and discussed the details at length.

After about an hour the driver returned. He started the engine and the car moved on again. Edna was certain they were driving through towns she knew because the number of times they stopped could only mean they were hitting traffic lights. For some reason they were not using highways. At one of the traffic lights the three men began discussing just when and where they would rape her.

"There's no use in waiting," the fat man said angrily to the two men in front.

"Don't rush," the driver said. "We're almost there."

Edna estimated that she had been in the car six or seven hours. She had no idea where she was, but she knew that she had to do something pretty soon. She had long ago stopped struggling and the fat man had stopped mauling her for a while.

"I've got to go to a rest room," she suddenly shouted.

"Wha?"

"I've got to go to a rest room. Fast!"

"Shee!"

"Let 'er go. I don't want her pissing all over me," one of the men in the front said.

After some grumbling among them the car slowed down and stopped in a shabby industrial area on the outskirts of Charlotte. The rest room was part of a factory complex and the area seemed deserted. The fat man got out of the car and pulled Edna out by an arm. He pressed a knife to the small of her back. As they approached the rest room the door suddenly opened and a large, middle-aged woman with two children in tow emerged. As her children walked on ahead, the woman held the door open for Edna. This confused the fat man and he stopped short of the door. Edna kept going. She quickly locked the rest room door. A window over the sink was unlocked. She boosted herself onto the sink and climbed through the window. The minute her feet hit the pavement she began running as fast as she could. She heard the three men shouting, but she did not turn around. She ran through vacant lots and over railroad tracks. Abruptly, she found a row of one-story buildings. She tried four or five doors until one of them opened. An elderly janitor was in the dimly lit lobby and it was he who called the police.

Twenty-two years. They had been married twenty-two years. They had started out in the basement of a two-family house in Flatbush, while he finished his internship. His first office was paid for by her parents. He never even thanked them. Mrs. Nancy Stein, the wife of Robert Stein, M.D., internist, heart specialist, and resident physician at Bronx Lebanon Hospital, was pouring out her story to her attorney. Nancy Stein was bitter. She had been separated from her doctor husband for about a year. Their son Charles was twenty and finishing Harvard; Gail was nineteen and a junior at Radcliffe. Meryl, fourteen, a freshman at a Westchester high school, continued to live with her mother in the family's eleven-room Hartsdale house. It was all agreeable at first. Robert was very busy. His practice was everything. He played squash. His life was regimented. He had time and room for everything but her. They quarreled. When he finally said he was going to move out for a while so things could calm down, she was almost happy. She suddenly felt free. Nancy did not think of it as a separation. To her it felt like a vacation. He came back once or twice a week to pick up Meryl and take her to the movies or to a restaurant. Things went on like that for a couple of months; then money problems began. For the first time since their marriage he began complaining about the cost of things. Her expenses were too high. She was spending too much on clothes. Even when she told him the clothes were for the children, not for her, it did not seem to matter. The money arguments continued and then, without any warning, he began cutting off her credit cards. First American Express went, then Mastercharge, BankAmericard, and the department stores—Saks Fifth Avenue, Bonwit Teller, and Lord and Taylor. The only thing he left her were her gasoline credit cards. He would give her a check every week. When it was not enough, she had to ask him for more.

Nancy Stein chain-smoked Camels and sipped mulled wine as she poured out her story to her attorney. She was afraid that he would cut her off completely. She had heard from the wives of doctors with whom he worked that he had begun seeing a nurse from Thailand who was supposed to be a Suzy Wong sort of knockout. Nancy Stein said she understood that he was trying to recapture something. At forty he began playing more squash and dressing like a younger man and he had bought his first sports car. It was all so pathetic. She suspected that the new girl friend might be one of the reasons why he was cutting back on his family obligations and she was afraid he was so unstable emotionally that he might try and divorce her and leave her without a cent. She wanted no more of it. She wanted to beat him to a divorce and make sure he could not hide his assets. He had always done the banking, and claimed to have less money than she knew was the case. Over the years she had gathered a fairly good idea of what he should now be worth. She had rummaged through the house and amassed check stubs and old credit cards and bank statements and old income tax forms. She wanted to be ready for the divorce. She had helped in putting together the comfortable life they had been living and she saw no reason, now that he was about to enter into his second childhood, that she should be denied anything. She wanted her fair share of any settlement.

"Getting a divorce," the lawyer said, "is like giving birth. It's hard work for a year."

The first step, of course, was to get together as much accurate information about her husband as possible. There had to be double checks on his income, his bank accounts, and, if he wanted to fight the matter in court, enough information about his extramarital sexual exploits to prove Mrs. Stein wounded and denied.

"You're going to have to hire a private detective to look into all of this," said the attorney.

Mrs. Ann Campbell did not know she lived in a slum. To her, 1050 Tiffany Street in the South Bronx was home. The uncollected garbage that piled up outside each apartment was strewn throughout the halls and onto the street. Rats scurried along the battered tile floors of the five-story tenement and late at night their tiny nails scratched out their routes. Many of the buildings in the area had been burned out; others were boarded up and abandoned. Mrs. Campbell's building had long ago been abandoned by the owners and taken over by the city. Idle young black and Puerto Rican men sat on the crumbling stoops or stared blankly at the eviscerated cars that rusted at the curbs. Rib-skinny dogs roamed wild and snarled at anyone, man or beast, who approached them while they foraged for scraps amid the bursting garbage.

Mrs. Campbell, who moved north from South Carolina fifty-three years ago, rarely left her neighborhood. Over the years she had forgotten that there were places that were not like Tiffany Street. She knew, though, that she was poor. Most of her life she had been on welfare. Her husband had left her more than twenty years earlier, but she had tried keeping her family together nevertheless.

On November 24, however, the day before Thanksgiving, Mrs. Campbell was even less disposed than usual to ruminate upon her woes. She was not going to fret about the trouble she was getting from the welfare people and she was not going to worry about the letter she received from the city that questioned her daughters' welfare payments. She also tried not to think about the boiling water that had been pouring from her bathtub faucet for three months. She had complained at the rent office many times, but the woman in charge of collecting the rent kept saying that the plumber was busy and that Lester

Roland, the building's superintendent, would fix the leak. Les kept telling Mrs. Campbell that the job needed the work of a real plumber, and that nothing could be done. They took her $250-a-month welfare rent subsidy check readily enough, but when it came to doing anything to improve the apartment nobody did anything. The electrical wiring, for instance, was so botched in her five-room apartment that the few working outlets were overloaded with added sockets, and extension cords wound their way through every room, draped across the tops of opened doors, twisted around ceiling fixtures and bursting forth, finally, in bare-bulb brilliance.

The spaghetti of extension cords, however, was only a minor inconvenience for Mrs. Campbell. The rats bothered her more. The fear of being burned alive in case of fire also haunted her. She had had to bar and padlock all of the windows in her fourth-floor apartment in an effort to keep out junkie burglars. But the cheap locks and gates had long ago rusted and Mrs. Campbell knew it would be impossible for her to escape if a fire broke out. She could not afford new gates and locks, however, so this was another fear she had learned to live with. But no matter how badly her flesh crawled at the scratchy noise of rats' nails on hallway tiles or how paralyzing was the choice between burglary or immolation, it was the steaming torrent of boiling water gushing from her ruptured bathtub faucet that frightened her the most. She had first complained about the water to the superintendent seven months before, but he said he couldn't do anything about the problem. Les had tried.

He had managed to shut it off for a couple of days, but then suddenly it would begin running again.

In order to stem the torrent, Mrs. Campbell had to turn off the apartment's main water valve underneath the bathroom sink. Whenever she turned off the main valve, of course, she was without any hot water anywhere. When she wanted to wash dishes in the kitchen she would have to open the main valve under the bathroom sink. Boiling water immediately gushed into the bathtub, but it was the only way she was able to use hot water. Mrs. Campbell was also frightened of using the main valve too often. Whenever she reached under the bathroom sink, spatters of boiling water splashed out of the steaming tub and struck her arms, face, neck, and legs. Sometimes she would try to cover herself with a towel or a sheet. Furthermore, she was no longer a supple woman and the contortions necessary to turning off the hot water added to her difficulties.

The situation was so bad that when the building's boiler was stoked the boiling water would begin overflowing the tub and swamping the bathroom floor. The apartment directly beneath Mrs. Campbell had been abandoned long ago and the torrent had forced the tenants on the second floor to abandon one end of their apartment and to use the bathroom of another abandoned apartment on the same floor. The intensity of the heat and billowing steam was such that thirty years' worth of laminated wallpaper was peeling off in layers like sliced baloney.

On November 24 the hot water had been pouring into

the bathtub all day long. Ann Campbell was fixing Thanksgiving dinner for her son, John, her two daughters, Ruth and Helen, and her seven grandchildren. She had propped a door in front of the bathroom in order to keep her toddling grandchildren from wandering in. At eight o'clock that night, most of her kitchen preparations completed for the day, Mrs. Campbell went to the bathroom with her daughter to turn off the main valve. She removed the door and started into the bathroom when she realized that the bathroom floor was about an inch deep in almost boiling water. Steam billowed out of the tub and filled the entire room. As she kneeled down under the sink to begin fiddling with the knob, Mrs. Campbell felt her feet begin to slide out from under her. She tried to stop from sliding, but she could not. Before she could grab a support she toppled over toward the bathtub filled with scalding water. Somehow she managed to hold on to the side of the tub with her left arm but her right arm and the right side of her head and torso slid beneath the boiling water. As she came out of the water, propped up by her left arm, she screamed.

2

"I'm the last resort. By the time they get to me they've been to the cleaners. They've been through all of the friends of friends and the cousins and Uncle Charlie who knows this lawyer and Eddie down the block who had the same thing happen to him, and finally the corporation lawyer who is supposed to know how to get things done, and then the brother always knows a guy who used to be a cop but there was some trouble back there that had to do with money or booze. And finally, when they find out that even the Godfathers are only in the movies, finally when they have absolutely nowhere else to go, when the gypsy fortune tellers have rolled the rugs onto the roof of the Eldorado and have disappeared over the George Washington Bridge, then they come to me, then I get them."

Irwin Blye is a private detective, a real private detective. He has been one for twenty of his forty-two years. He serves as a bodyguard, advisor, and guide to clients enmeshed in the loophole madness of the judicial process. His primary job is to ease his clients through a system that is characterized by indifference, corruption, and sloppy paperwork. The bank robbers, mafia bosses, crooked congressmen, and corrupt cops he has occasionally represented can learn a trick or two from him.

He is hired by banks to find debt skippers who owe more than $10,000. He is employed by businessmen to find out which of their trusted employees is robbing them blind and which of their partners is juggling the books. Insurance companies hire him in suspicious negligence cases that require more talent at detection than is generally employed in their own offices. In insurance fraud cases Blye has spent weeks trying to trick claimants out of their feigned ailments. He has put weights in their garbage cans or given them flat tires and then photographed them carrying out the garbage or fixing flats to prove that their multimillion-dollar incapacitation suits are fake.

Blye has located everything from house pets and diamond necklaces to small children and senile grandparents. He has been called in by embittered heirs who want to break wills and by embittered husbands and wives who want to break up marriages. Politicians have hired him to uncover dirt in rival campaigns and, at times, Blye has had the distinct impression that the pols wouldn't have minded at all if he had planted a little dirt in the rival's closet.

Private detectives are nowhere mentioned in the official charters addressing themselves to the majesty of the law. Men like Irwin Blye are not part of the clubby law-school-and-black-robe set. Rather, Irwin Blye is a representative of the back rooms off the halls of justice. He is the shrewd middleman of America's judicial process. He is permitted to operate between the spirit and the letter of the nation's impenetrable and often unenforceable laws. Unofficially, therefore, Irwin Blye is certified to move in the cracks of the nation's criminal justice system, thus absolving its loftier members of the need for contact with some of the seedier aspects of their profession.

Merriam-Webster III defines the private investigator as a person "concerned with the maintenance of lawful conduct or the investigation of a crime or other irregularities either as the regular employee of a private interest (as a hotel or store) or as a contractor for fees. . . ."

New York State, which licenses more than seven thousand private investigators, delineates at great length the functions of the profession:

> . . . to obtain information about crimes committed anywhere in the country and investigate and identify the habits, conduct, whereabouts, affiliations, reputations and character of any person or group; can find missing persons; can locate and recover lost and stolen property; can find the causes and

origins and investigate the validity of legal actions that come as the result of fires, libel suits, accidents; and whose testimony can be used before any authorized investigating committee, board of award, board of arbitration or trial in civil or criminal cases.

The real world of the private detective has little to do with tidy definitions. Blye's is a world in which court clerks take $2 from busy cops to call their cases early; where kickbacks among lawyers, accountants, and investigators are common; where judges are sometimes so drunk that they confuse the defendants with the complainants and court clerks have to forge their signatures in order to keep bewildered victims of robberies from being carted off to jail. It is a world in which perjury, politics, and payoffs often dictate verdicts, and testimony of witnesses, including cops, is casually bargained for in the corridors and toilets of the court moments before trial. It is a world in which true guilt and innocence are meaningless, where the words are defined by the guile of the attorneys rather than the actual condition of the accused.

From his very first day as a private detective, Irwin Blye has found that the criminal and civil justice system is essentially a marketplace in which insiders—prison guards, bondsmen, court clerks, lawyers, prosecutors, judges, even the reporters who cover the courts—play elaborate and dazzling games with the uninitiated. From car crashes to murder, everything is for sale.

"Sometimes during a court break I'll see a lawyer go out the side door with an assistant district attorney or

shake his hand or put his arm on the guy's back, even if
he doesn't really know the guy all that well," Blye says.

"Then later he'll go over to his client, the defendant,
who has been watching all this like his life depended
upon it, and it probably did. The lawyer is playing it all
hush-hush. He tells the client that it's okay. It's in the
bag. He's got a misdemeanor plea if worse comes to
worst. He'd get that anyway, but the client doesn't know
it. The lawyer then says it'll cost another $1,500 or an-
other $5,000, depending upon what the traffic will bear.
The client always gets the money up and the lawyer
always pockets it clean. No taxes. No payoffs. No nothing. The young assistant district attorneys soon catch on,
however, and it's fun for me to watch them dancing
around the courtroom during recess so that they are not
caught in a position where they get their backs slapped
by defense counsel.

"On the streets and in the courtrooms," Blye continues, "it's all very different from the books and the television shows and movies. And I don't only mean the lawyers pretending to bribe cops and prosecutors and
pocketing the cash payoffs turned over by their own clients. It's one thing to watch Kojak read somebody his
rights on Sunday night and for the Supreme Court to
insist upon knock-knock, but when a pair of street cops
grab somebody for something, take my word for it, it is
quite some time before he hears his rights. Usually the
first time the prisoner is aware that he has had rights read
to him is just before the trial when the arresting officer
goes through his catechism testimony crossing every 't'

and dotting every 'i.' And when a couple of bulls have to go into a room after somebody, believe me, the door goes first and then comes the knock-knock."

Most of Irwin Blye's time is spent with criminal, matrimonial, and insurance negligence cases. Unlike the private detectives of fiction, who sit around grubby offices waiting to defend the wrongly accused, Irwin Blye usually finds himself in the employ of attorneys searching for ways to keep their clients out of jail, strange beds, or permanent traction.

In criminal cases, the role of the private investigator is not so much one of catching crooks as it is of freeing them. He is part of an elaborate adversary game between prosecutors and defense attorneys, in which a defendant's freedom is determined by the outcome of a courtroom contest rather than his guilt or innocence. In that game it is Irwin Blye's responsibility to find flaws in the prosecutor's case and to give the defense attorney enough information so that the charges against his client can be either dismissed or reduced. The private detective, therefore, talks to everyone with whom the police have talked. He questions the same witnesses and looks for additional witnesses who might contradict those lined up on the prosecutor's side. He visits the scene of the crime and measures distances between safes and doors and windows and tries to reconstruct as accurately as possible the evidence submitted to the court by the police, looking for discrepancies—any doorway, air conditioning duct, or stairway that might cast doubt on the conclusions drawn by the district attorney from police reports.

Private detectives will often go inside the jails in which their clients are held to talk with them about possible alibis and to get leads on additional witnesses who might testify on their behalf. On retrials and appeals, private investigators will talk to jurors and try to determine exactly what the weaknesses were in their client's original case, trying always to find the faults in the defense that the attorneys can then correct.

A recent example of such activities was Blye's efforts to free Jerry O'Conner, a man accused of armed bank robbery. O'Conner claimed he was not the holdup man. He insisted it was a matter of mistaken identity. The police, in their plodding, thorough manner, had interviewed every person and storekeeper on the block where the holdup took place. Cops are, after all, civil servants working on civil servants' time. The cost to most private citizens of duplicating or double-checking police facts on a detective's D.D. 5 is usually prohibitive. In this case, though, the defendant's family had some money and it could afford Blye's fee. O'Conner's lawyer gave Blye the Police Department's report (it is a normal legal procedure in most courts for the prosecutor to show the defense the nature of the evidence against his client) and Blye began his trek. First there was Mrs. Feder in the dress shop, from which the holdup victims first called the police, because the crooks had cut the phone lines in the bank.

"Did they tell you what happened? Did they describe the holdup team?"

Then there was the Wha Wah Restaurant, next door, Helen Rosen Lingerie, Rose's Stationery, Tacker TV, Volo Restaurant, Wald's Supermarket, Beman's Meat Market, Riker's Bake Shop, Cole Fisheries, Bride & Groom Sales, Deep Barber Shop, Dole Drug Store, a nameless luncheonette, Carl's Shoe Repair, a travel bureau, a U.S. post office, Dr. Hessler's office, a deli, the E. H. Polk residence, the Barbara Melufo residence, a cleaners and a Shell gas station as well as the witnesses in the bank.

To some it would be tedious work but to Irwin Blye, looking for the witness who didn't go along with the police version, it is challenging.

"I am nosy," he says. "I've always been nosy. I enjoy the work. The police have to tell you what they did, but they don't have to tell you that somebody in the shoe repair shop and the gas station gave a different description of the holdup man. You've got to find that out for yourself and you've got to talk them into helping.

"Your average bank robber is really pretty demented," Blye continues, "so Jerry O'Conner's elaborate alibi right away stuck in my head. Bank robbers don't usually have alibis. Most of them are the kinds of guys who leave their wallets behind. I once had two guys who staked out a bank for a week from the grocery store across the street. One of them insisted upon wearing a cowboy hat and red shirt and he kept yelling to a third guy in a car outside, asking if he wanted a sandwich or soda from the grocery. By the middle of the week the local storeowners had a pool going on the exact day and time of the bank heist.

"I had another guy who took his ski mask off during the middle of the robbery because the bank manager said he couldn't make out the instructions. O'Conner was different. He was dopey, but not that dopey. He had done time for a previous bank robbery, but on this one he said he was clean. Sitting in prison awaiting trial he had reconstructed to the finest detail everything he had done that day in order to prove he couldn't have been holding up the bank when the cops said he was."

O'Conner told Blye that on the day of the bank robbery, a Friday, he had cashed his workmen's compensation check in a branch bank near the New York Coliseum where he had worked as a freight handler, moving exposition material around. After wrenching his back during the hardware show, he began getting $176 every two weeks. He remembered on that particular Friday first trying to cash the check in the Plaza Cafe, but since it was too early in the day—about eleven o'clock in the morning—the owner didn't have enough cash to cover the check. O'Conner then went across the street to the bank where his former employer had an account and, after having his check approved by the manager, he cashed it. Then he got into his car, which he had parked in the Coliseum garage, and drove home.

"The timing of all this was such that it would have been impossible for Jerry to have been holding up a bank on Long Island when he was cashing a check in midtown

Manhattan," Blye says, "except it had all happened months before and who do you know can remember one Friday payday from another that long ago?

"First thing you do is subpoena a copy of the check O'Conner remembered cashing that day from the insurance company that handled the Coliseum's compensation cases. When the trial begins O'Conner's lawyer is able to do that through the court. Most people forget that lawyers are officers of the court. They can subpoena just about anything, including a ham sandwich, if they think it is relevant to the defense of their clients. Next, you subpoena the New York Police Department to produce everything they have in the case. You get their photographs of the defendant and of the crime scene, you get records of the police alarms and the various descriptions of the holdup men broadcast during the day. You get the records of the descriptions as given by witnesses and you get the names, addresses, and occupation of the witnesses.

"In this case," Blye continues, "we also subpoenaed the records of the Mobil Oil Corporation. Not all of their records, just the records and time sheets for the day of the holdup from the Coliseum garage, which Mobil ran. We also got a medical report from the Workmen's Compensation Board as to the exact nature of O'Conner's injury.

"You get, in other words, as much information as you can. Everything. And then, sometimes, the pieces begin to fit. Sometimes the client's excuses and alibis are substantiated. Most of the time, a client's alibi turns out to be more damaging than the evidence the cops have amassed, but in the case of Jerry O'Conner things dovetailed.

"For instance," Blye goes on, "the workmen's comp check he cashed was cashed on the same day as the stickup. In the case of most clients the day would have been a little off. Usually, clients aren't aware of the power of a subpoena and how all of that vague stuff they think exists out there in the bureaucracy can be brought right back to face them in court. Most clients wouldn't know you could retrieve a six-month-old workmen's comp check.

"Now, if I could prove that the time the check was cashed was about the same time of the stickup his chances in court would improve tremendously. Especially since the bank official who had endorsed it was the branch manager and among the notations he made for identification purposes was a driver's license and a municipal golf course membership card. When I checked O'Conner's driver's license and golf card, both had passport photos of O'Conner on them, making the chance for a false identification on the part of the bank manager remote.

"If I could also get the garage records to show that his car was parked in the Coliseum garage during the period he said he was cashing his check, that would also help. The garagemen, however, weren't too much help, but it took me hours to find that out. The garage had two levels and a capacity of about 850 cars. While there was a record that a car with O'Conner's license plate had been driven into the garage at 10:40 A.M. on the morning of the bank robbery—again corroborating O'Conner's story—due to a garage screwup there was no record of his car ever having left the garage. This is typical of the kinds of things, real things, that happen in police work all the time, but somehow never get on television.

"When O'Conner pulled his car out of the garage, the parking garage attendant had apparently pulled the wrong card out of the rack and used it to clock out O'Conner's car. When the customer whose ticket the attendant had confused with O'Conner's drove out, the attendant realized he didn't have a ticket for him in the rack. According to Mike Waters, the garage man, the attendant then made out an emergency ticket for the car. At the end of the day when all of the other cars had checked out, the only ticket left in the rack was O'Conner's. What that did, of course, was blow O'Conner's timing excuse out of the water, but it helped me. It gave me the odd feeling that maybe O'Conner was telling the truth. It may not have helped him in court, but it made me want to dig a little bit harder.

"I began to look at the descriptions of the bank's holdup man," Blye continues. "I noticed that the police had focused on O'Conner right away. He was a big man. About six feet three inches and weighing 250 pounds. When I talked to the bank employees who gave the police descriptions of the man, I realized that the detectives had pulled one of the old dirty tricks. They had put the witnesses before the mug shot book and turned the pages. Every so often a picture of O'Conner would turn up. After a while the person going through book after book of photographs begins to see O'Conner in his sleep. It's the original subliminal sell. Cops don't do that unless they are really interested in making a case against somebody. So I began to poke around and find out why.

"It turned out that the reason the cops really wanted O'Conner had nothing to do with the bank robbery. He was a close pal of a rogue cop named Neal and the department probably had an illegal wire on Neal's telephone. During a conversation about another stickup, O'Conner asked Neal what he should do if a patrolman walked onto the scene. 'Blow him away,' the rogue cop told O'Conner, and that was all the police had to hear. Since their wire was not legal they couldn't use the information in court, but they were hoping to get O'Conner on a bank robbery and then squeeze him into implicating his pal Neal for a lighter sentence. The cops really wanted Neal, and O'Conner was the pigeon they planned to use to get him.

When the case finally went to trial and I had the bank officials testify that O'Conner had been cashing a check at the time of the robbery and substantiate that fact by the numbered sequence used to keep tabs of the checks cashed in a bank during the day, the police were really annoyed that we had done our homework. We even had the Workmen's Compensation doctor come into court and testify that O'Conner had lost almost all the strength in his right arm as a result of the accident and could not possibly have vaulted the bank rail toward the safe as all of the robbery witnesses had testified. The only problem with the doctor was that I had to stay up all night with him keeping him sober so that he could testify in the morning. We got O'Conner off and the cops had to get Neal another way."

Matrimonial cases are another arena in which the courts, the lawyers, and the private investigators play their elaborate games. In the old door-busting days when adultery was the only reason for which New York divorces were granted, dramatic bedroom confrontations were often concocted with witnesses, cameras, disheveled sheets, and private detectives recording the "illicit" affairs. Today, adultery is no longer the only grounds for divorce in New York, but that does not mean that the private detective and his peephole tricks have been abandoned. Business is booming. In New York alone there are approximately fifty thousand divorces processed through the civil courts every year. They make up half of all the cases that appear in the civil courts, almost two hundred of them a day. While the majority of them move along smoothly enough, there are still thousands of cases that involve litigation. Alimony and child support disputes invariably require the services of shrewd lawyers and private eyes.

"He doesn't want to pay and says he's broke," Blye explains. "She says he's loaded and is hiding his income. That's just about all of them in a nutshell."

A "no fault" divorce essentially means that both parties agree to a separation and one year later either one of them is entitled to convert that separation into a divorce. Instead of the wars that used to be fought over the divorce procedures, today the real battle is over the separation agreements. Raoul Lionel Felder, one of the nation's most successful divorce lawyers, for whom Blye often works, is very frank about the game:

"If it comes to a fight, it is the lawyer's function, using all ethical, legal, and moral means, to bring his adversary to his knees as fast as possible. Naturally, within this framework the lawyer must go for the 'soft spots.' "

Seated behind a large antique desk in his damask-walled Fifth Avenue office, Raoul Lionel Felder tries to give the impression of not having very many soft spots himself. On his desk, for instance, holding his freshly sharpened pencils, is an empty Bon Vivant soup can. Bon Vivant, one recalls, was the brand name of the tainted vichyssoise that killed several people a few years ago.

"The private investigators we use," Felder says, "are extremely important to our cases. We have to be able to trust them. A private detective who can be bought by the other side or later uses stuff he picks up in the investigation to blackmail clients is the kind of man we try to avoid."

Felder smiles, conscious of the dramatic contrast between his demeanor and the outrageous subject of his conversation. Raoul Lionel Felder is a litigator. He is a theatrical figure who comes alive before the footlights of the courts. His clients tend to be wealthy and powerful. Recently he represented a bishop in the Episcopal Diocese of New York in a divorce action and charged in court that the bishop's wife of twenty-four years became infatuated with the manager of an ice cream parlor and had an "open, wanton, and notorious relationship" with the man. The tabloids loved the story. Raoul Lionel Felder plays rough, and he takes particular delight in a client who enjoys the work as much as he does.

"Some people just take to it," he says. "They're geniuses. One man I know who suspected his wife was having an affair with a family friend, without telling me, before I was retained, actually conned the guy into believing he didn't really care. In a sense, I suppose, he didn't care. But he cared enough to want a divorce and he cared enough for the divorce not to cost him a cent. So, the guy became chummy as hell with his wife's lover. Finally, he's got a tape recorder going in the apartment and he says, very calmly and matter of factly, 'I know you're screwing my wife, but I don't care.'

"The guy was a little taken aback, but when he sees that his pal is not angry he says that he's glad the husband sees it that way. But the guy is a genius. He wants more than that. He needs some kind of statement that gets the lover to admit he has had sex with his wife. So, he begins talking about whether they are serious and if he should get a lawyer and they begin to commiserate on some of the wife's faults. The husband goes on at great length about how it hadn't worked for either of them sexually for quite a while. The lover was sympathetic. The husband then began talking about his inadequacies sexually, that it would probably never be any good for him. I listened to the tape. It was a virtuoso performance. It brought tears to the eyes. Finally, his wife's lover couldn't stand any more of the husband's self-doubt and said the words the husband had been hoping to hear. He said, 'Marty, I don't know what you're so worried about. She was like a corpse. She's the one with the problem. I didn't even enjoy it.' "

Raoul Lionel Felder loves the story. With more clients like that he wouldn't need detectives. But most of his clients are not quite so cold-blooded during personal crises, such as their own divorces, and Raoul Lionel Felder has to rely on the work of private detectives.

"Depending upon what you need," he says, "that's where you go. Financial reporting services are okay, but they don't give you the detail needed. Former post office inspectors who work as private investigators are usually good workers. They usually know everything about neighborhoods, even tough neighborhoods like Bedford-Stuyvesant. I know some postal guys who are just great. The big companies are good for some things, but I don't go for them in divorce work. All they really do is send girls out to county clerk offices looking for previous litigation involving the subject. No, you need more than that.

"Irwin Blye puts most of these things together," Felder continues. "He knows the law and that is a tremendous help. He knows what we need, knows what to look for, and knows how to get it in such a way that we can present it in a court of law. He also seems to get on with people. He always gets the help he needs. Whether it's from a real estate office or a hotel clerk, men and women seem to help him. And then, he's honest. If he says he worked eight hours on a job with two men, that's what he did. Every once in a while you get a yo-yo client who wants to see the two detectives she is paying for. With Blye you know they will be there. And, also, there is the matter of perjury. If the private detective's affidavit says that there were two investigators who saw the couple go into the motel and it turns out there was only one man present, that can make trouble for a case. That's why I use Blye. I know where I stand. I know when I go into court with data compiled by Irwin, I'm not going to get any nasty surprises.

"And then," Felder says, "Blye doesn't screw around with the clients. That's almost an occupational disease with some of these privates. They think it goes with the territory. The women they are working for during a divorce are often emotionally upset. They get daily reports about how their husbands are screwing around and there is the great big private detective telling her all of this stuff and he's got a gun and it will all be a part of the past pretty soon. Next thing you know your client is in bed with your detective and sooner or later she's going to decide that she was used and that she doesn't feel she has to pay the rest of her bill. It happens every time. With Blye I don't have to worry. I don't know why. Maybe he's too smart. I don't know. One thing about Irwin, however. He's kind to them all."

"Instead of spending all my time looking into motel bedrooms," Blye later says, "I find that I'm spending more and more time checking into a man's net worth. I check with the county clerk where he lives and where he does business to see what outstanding litigation there is against him. I check with his business partners, his clients, his competitors, and suppliers in an attempt to put together an honest value on his holdings. The eventual settlement, the child support, all of the things that will come out of the divorce will be based on the evaluation of the man's worth. He'll be stuck with those payments forever."

Custody of children is another part of the divorce drama that often requires the services of the private investigator.

"My job is to get custody for my client," one divorce attorney explains, with a verve typical of the profession. "And that's what I'll do, even if I have to trap the wife in a motel with some guy to do it."

Divorce lawyers and their private investigators use every legal trick they know and some other barely legal ones as well. They bury their opponents in procedural motions that turn into a blizzard of paper. They will hound, harass, and intimidate the opposition and they will suggest as delicately as possible that their own clients help out with little white lies, the concealing of assets—even hiding their children.

Recently, Seward Prosser Mellon, heir to the Pittsburgh banking fortune, one of the world's great fortunes, was given custody of his two daughters by a Pennsylvania court and his ex-wife was given custody of the same two daughters by a New York court. The children's mother, Karen Boyd Mellon, immediately hired a private detective firm to protect the two girls. Her intention was, of course, to remain within the New York boundaries where she had custody of her children. Meanwhile, the girls' father, the Pittsburgh banker, hired another New York private detective firm in the hopes of getting his daughters back to Pennsylvania where a Pittsburgh judge had given him custody.

The next thing that happened was that the two girls were abducted in broad daylight as they were leaving their Brooklyn home on their way to school. Their mother's private detective was apparently overpowered by three men suspected of being their father's private detectives, and the children were whisked away. Mr. Mellon's attorneys deny that any kidnapping or illegal activity of any kind was used, but they do admit that their client, the girls' father, does now have custody of the children.

"Whether custody cases or money settlements," Blye says, "almost all matrimonials wind up in peek-a-boo and from that point on they become repetitive.

"Even the cheating itself takes on certain patterns," Blye continues. "Women, for instance, always cheat during the week. Wednesdays and Thursday nights are their biggest cheating nights. They are usually able to use the excuse of a card party, a bingo parlor, or even that they're going shopping in a store that stays open late. They always use as their excuse something that is a part of the family living pattern. She'll go to the bingo parlor or card party or go shopping. She'll even buy something and then go on to her lover. Some of these affairs that have been going on for a while have almost become second marriages. They use the same pattern. They be-

gin to feel safe. They use the same motels. They begin
to get comfortable. They begin to meet in the same
shopping center parking lot. The woman will often get
there first. She'll do some shopping and then wait for the
guy. She'll often call her husband during the wait.

" 'Hi, honey, I'm at Macy's. I see some nice socks. Do
you need socks?'

"The woman will have left her house right after dinner
and a call from the store allays any suspicion. She gets
home about an hour after the stores close, usually by
eleven.

"While the woman is going through her shopping ritual, her boyfriend is preregistering in the motel. These
guys almost always check in under phony names, but in
court they can be identified by their handwriting. The
man usually pays cash and once he's registered he has
the room key in his pocket and there is no need to register while the woman waits in the car. At the end of the
evening the man drives the woman back to where she has
left her car at the parking lot and there's always a little
good-night kiss.

"For the men," Blye goes on, "it's much easier. They
just don't go home after work. It's easier for a man to
come home with liquor on his breath. He has freedom.
He's not stuck in the house like his wife. It's the old
business meeting gambit, and even if his wife is suspicious, what the hell can she do? Sometimes driving
through the east side of Manhattan between Fifth and
York and from the sixties to the nineties, I'll see a dozen
private investigators outside apartments, sitting on jobs.

"Hardly anyone uses the hotels in Manhattan," Blye says. "Everyone prefers motels. They use the Fairway, near the Hudson River, or the Oceanside near Queens Boulevard, or the Edgemere near Jericho Turnpike. The Howard Johnson motels discourage people by asking for luggage and asking how long you plan to stay. The other places, though, are known as 'hot bed' joints. They have no bellhops and doormen poking around. It costs a fast $16 to $22 for the room. Some of these motels have a whole section that they turn over to the hot bed people and other rooms set aside for the all-night legitimate guests. Lots of times the managers in these hot bed motels will rent the rooms out to couples for a couple of hours and pocket the cash. The motel management never knows that he has sent a number of couples through the room while charging up only one customer for the night.

"Also, hot bed motels are not necessarily crummy places at all," Blye explains. "They are often very good motels and they fully understand the nature of much of their business and the peculiar needs that their special customers require. The Edgemere out near Jericho Turnpike, for instance, put up a fence to hide the license plates and most of the cars parked outside the motel rooms. They also installed a wooden box with a slot into which you can drop your key when you check out of the motel after paying in advance. In these kinds of places they discourage people like me from poking around. They'll often call the police, and the cops ask us not to make trouble. We understand that the cops are usually

(36)

taken care of by the motel owners, and we try to avoid any kind of confrontation with the police.

"When you finally get what the lawyers need—and that doesn't mean X-rated snapshots, just an established and suspicious pattern of meeting in motel rooms for specific periods of time and a parting kiss—some of the less scrupulous lawyers always want you to exaggerate. They want us to push the time they left the motel to past midnight, instead of 11:30 P.M. The reason for that is that when the lawyer takes the case to court he is able to accuse the woman or man of having left the house on one day and returned the next. 'You left on Wednesday and returned on Thursday,' he'll say. Lots of lawyers like that overnight bit so much that they want their private detectives to perjure themselves to make it true. Another thing the lawyers are always after private investigators to exaggerate is the good-night kiss. I suppose I've seen thousands of good-night kisses between parting lovers, and the great number of those kisses were planted square on the cheek. The lawyers like you to write up your reports to say that 'the male and subject kissed on the lips.' Experienced lawyers, however, know that divorces are granted when there is established an opportunity and the inclination for an adulterous act. The opportunity simply means two people alone in either an apartment or motel for a couple of hours during either the evening or night.

"No third parties allowed. The court will throw a case out if the couple can prove that a third party was present. By today's X-rated standards three-in-a-bed is legit, but two can't go."

Negligence is another area in which the private investigator prospers. He is forever checking up on the extent of injuries, real or supposed, as well as taking statements from any and all witnesses to the accidents that are serving as the basis for damage suits. Much of this work, however, is done by the kind of private detective who has a long and valued relationship with the government agency that originally recorded the accident, such as the cops. The business gets ethically murky, because it has been a common practice among shrewd cops to hold out the names of potentially good witnesses when making up their accident reports. Later, when the insurance investigator or the adjustor, usually an ex-cop, shows up at the precinct looking for the accident reports, the names of potentially good witnesses can be sold for between $25 and $50 each.

Things in the "whiplash" trade, as the negligence field is known to those in the business, were so bad in New York City for a while that cops assigned to the Accident Investigations Unit, the men who take the pictures of crashes, measure skid marks, talk to survivors, etc., would sell their reports to the insurance companies by the length of the skid marks. A twenty-yard skid could cost the insurance investigator $100 for a copy of the report. Additional witnesses were, of course, extra. One of the reasons insurance companies use former cops for this kind of work is that the police are far more likely to sell their information to ex-cops or ex-partners than to a stranger.

If someone unknown walked into a precinct and off-

ered $5 a yard for accident information, the same cop
who might take the money from a guy he knew would
unquestionably lock up the stranger for attempted bribery.

And then there is the nasty business of recovering
stolen property. The men who recover those millions
upon millions of dollars of stolen typewriters, mink
coats, and jewelry for the insurance companies are almost always former police detectives who had worked in
the burglary squads. Recovering stolen goods is an area
that Irwin Blye prefers to avoid. It is too messy. The lines
between the burglar, the cops, the victims, and the insurance companies are far too blurred for even supremely
cynical types like Blye.

"That's a business where it doesn't pay to ask too
many questions," Blye says. "That doesn't mean you
can't look and see how peculiar the whole thing is, but
the more I look the less I want to get involved. A while
back, for instance, a well-known jewelry fence in the city
by the name of Romeo was arrested. Some stolen jewelry
from a hotel job had been traced to him and the burglary
squad guys called him on the phone and made an appointment for the arrest. He was that well known and
respected.

"When the detectives went to Romeo's warehouse
they found hundreds of earrings, brooches, Rolex wrist-
watches, diamond rings, emerald chokers, pearl necklaces. The works. He had the stuff stashed all over the
place. Crates, cartons, shoeboxes, Zabar shopping bags.
It was unbelievable. There was so much stuff stashed

around that place that the detectives decided they didn't have enough time to itemize every single piece of the jewelry they recovered. It was going to be too much paperwork—matching each item with a description and then trying to find a similar item somebody had reported stolen. None of that stuff is computerized. It would mean going through hundreds of thousands of property slips as well as writing up several thousand new property recovery slips. No way. Ninety-nine per cent of the people who lost that stuff had already gotten their money back from the insurance companies, anyway, so there wasn't any real incentive for the detectives to wind up getting writer's cramp.

"The detectives did what they usually do. They vouchered the recovered items in lots, instead of individually. They listed, for instance, 'fifty diamond earrings,' 'four gross Cartier watches,' that kind of thing. It was a reasonable decision for anyone who doesn't know how such things work. But the minute the cops decided not to itemize every single piece of jewelry recovered and chose not to find the owners of that stolen property, they were doing a professional fence a very big favor.

"What happens when the stolen property is not itemized is that the fence eventually gets it all back. It's a beautiful gambit and it works like this. Romeo is arrested by the detectives and is arraigned in court. A lawyer and bail bondsman are present so he's out on bail within a few hours. Then his lawyer starts plea-bargaining with the assistant district attorney over whether or not he should plead guilty. In this case Romeo kept up the plea-bargaining for nine months, out on bail all this time.

"Finally, his lawyer says to the ADA that Romeo will plead guilty to a criminal possession charge. The prosecutor accepts the plea and then, four months later, the judge gets around to sentencing Romeo to three years' probation. This means he walks.

"Romeo walked right out of that judge's court and across the street to the civil court where he initiated a lawsuit to get all that unclaimed jewelry, seized by the police at his warehouse, returned to him. Because he pleaded guilty, you see, he not only got the light sentence, but the cops didn't have to call any witnesses or complainants to testify against him. No one walked into the court and identified any of the jewelry found in his warehouse, because no one was ever notified by the police that the stolen property had been recovered. Within a couple of months Romeo got his swag from the court and was back in business."

3 T

RENTINO: I want a full detailed report on your investigation.

CHICO MARX: All right, I tell you. Monday we watch Firefly's house. But he no come out. He wasn't home. Tuesday we go to the ball game, but he fool us. He no show up. Wednesday he go to the ball game, and we fool him. We no show up. Thursday was a double header. Nobody show up. Friday it rained all day. There was no ball game, so we stayed home and we listened to it over the radio.

Duck Soup

Though you wouldn't know it from the way they are portrayed on television and in the movies, the majority of America's thirty-two thousand private investigators,

Blye, Private Eye

and that includes New York's seven thousand and Los
Angeles's five thousand, are not very good. Most are
retired cops supplementing their pensions by spending
two or three days a week walking to banks with nervous
businessmen. They are a plodding, part-time breed,
earning less than $7,500 a year and conditioned to en-
dure tedium. They watch over the children of the rich.
They patrol the aisles of department stores keeping an
eye on customers and sales personnel alike. They work
in hotels, where most of their time is spent ministering
to the tribulations of drunken guests. They double-check
claims against insurance companies, usually in the most
perfunctory way, such as calling the claimant's neighbor
and asking, point-blank, if he thinks his next-door neighbor is cheating on his injury claim. The private detective
may not come up with anything very startling with these
techniques, but he can note down the names and addresses of people interviewed in connection with the
case and get his $10-an-hour minimum private-eye fee.

Private eyes, for the most part, have always been little
more than handmaidens to the nation's lawyers.
Whether dealing in complicated estate cases, simple matrimonials, insurance scams, or seedy criminal defenses,
a lawyer needs the services of someone with at least a
rudimentary knowledge of the workings of the law and
a pal or two at police headquarters. The lawyer needs the
services of someone he can send out into the street to get
sworn statements, serve subpoenas, sign affidavits, interview potential witnesses, and, in a pinch, get coffee.

"We Never Sleep," was Alan Pinkerton's motto in
1849 when his trademark, a single wide-awake eye, de-

(43)

noted the nation's first successful private detective agency, and gave private eyes the nickname that has stuck ever since. The business of detecting for hire, however, has expanded far beyond Pinkerton's original duties—chasing the James Gang and breaking the heads of union organizers. Today, in fact, the private detective business is expanding at such a rate that most of those part-time former flatfoots, happy to pick up cigar money by peeking in keyholes, are finding less and less to do. They simply cannot keep up. Laws of search and seizure, pretrial evidentiary motions, and a whole thicket of complicated legal rulings have made most private investigators obsolete.

Much of the expansion in the private detective business has been in the industrial area, where more and more businesses are beginning to hire increasingly sophisticated firms to handle delicate corporate subjects such as industrial spying, investigations of prospective executive employees, and checks into the background of companies being considered as partners in planned mergers. The other major area of expansion has been in public defender cases. As a result of recent Supreme Court rulings dictating that all defendants are entitled to representation by counsel, the nation's courts have had to provide, at local, state, and federal expense, the services of defense attorneys to any defendant facing a possible jail term. The defense attorney, usually chosen from a list of lawyers approved by the local courts, is paid anywhere up to $500 for state cases and $750 for federal cases, depending upon the number of hours spent on the case.

The Supreme Court ruling that established a defendant's right to counsel also specified that the attorneys had the right to employ, also at government expense, the services of a private investigator to assist in the preparation of the defense. It was not a particularly well-known feature of the Court's ruling, but word spread quickly in the private detective business and increasing numbers of private eyes began taking on the defense of clients who could not have afforded them just a few years ago. Depending upon the state and the ruling of the local federal district judge, private investigators receive about $10 an hour for state cases or a maximum of about $300 per case. The work is drudgery for the most part. It entails double-checking the charges presented in the prosecution's case. Since prosecutors amass their cases from the clues and data compiled by their local police department, errors of fact are not at all uncommon. Without the private detective's independent inquiry, however, the defense attorney would have no way of knowing that the window through which the accused is supposed to have shot the storekeeper did not really exist.

"But my client couldn't have shot the victim through that window, ladies and gentlemen of the jury," Perry Mason says, smiling slyly at his full-time private investigator, "because there was no window in that wall."

"Not guilty," says the jury.

Reality does not work exactly that way, but it is close. The nation's police are actually not much more competent than anyone else in society. They do not catch crooks and prepare cases against them any better than television repairmen, automobile mechanics, and newspaper reporters go about their tasks. Error creeps in. Lazy cops feel they have enough evidence for their case and forget about interviewing other possible witnesses to the crime. The private detective is supposed to find those extra witnesses, check the details of the police reports, and generally pick apart the police case.

Instead of performing this role properly, however, many private detectives simply drop in on their old pals and former police comrades and copy their information straight from the investigation reports filed by the cops, thus diminishing by at least 100 per cent any chance of finding inaccuracies in the prosecutor's case. With more lawyers and greater interest in these criminal cases, however, incompetent and lazy private investigators are finding less and less employment.

The law, especially criminal law, is a complex matter. It is a tactician's game. The outcome of a trial, almost always determined by the cleverness and preparedness of the attorney, rather than the innocence or guilt of the defendant, has very little room for the old-fashioned part-time private eye. Nor is it a business that lends itself to the kind of spontaneous excursion into mystery-solving, sans attorney, that we have come to expect from Philip Marlowe and Harry Orwell. Today, most successful private investigators who work on criminal cases, the ambitious ones, at least, are doing more than just going through the simple routines of Xeroxing police department inquiries. Private detectives such as Irwin Blye clump from house to house, witness to witness, store to store, asking many of the same questions asked by the police who preceded them and, occasionally, coming up with different answers. In addition, today's private eyes have begun looking into the law books themselves. Irwin Blye, for instance, admits a fascination with the law and he claims that a private investigator who is not thoroughly familiar with the legal precedents, codes, rules of evidence, and the countless details of preparing a criminal defense is not really doing the job for which he is getting paid and is also missing out on half the fun.

"I am not a Harvard lawyer," Blye says, "and I admit that maybe I'm more interested in the law's loopholes than its foundations, but nowadays if you want to do more in my business than watch hotel lobbies you'd better get interested in the rules and regulations of the game itself."

The greatest explosion in the use of private investigators, however, has not come from the state-subsidized defense of defendants, but from the nation's corporations and the businessmen who want their competitors checked out, their errant daughters watched, their wives' drinking habits monitored, and their potential partners secretly scrutinized. The private detective agencies that deal with America's businessmen are certainly not the bottle-in-the-desk-drawer crowd. Rather, the agencies that cater to the new corporate clients are very much like the companies that employ them. There is little room for one-man operations, even talented one-man operations, such as Irwin Blye's. Big companies like to deal with big companies and, especially where overseas security work is concerned, the smaller private detective outfits cannot provide the kinds of services required.

Two of the nation's largest firms, Pinkerton and

Burns, do have the manpower and expertise to deal with almost any kind of corporate case, from the $10-to-$32-an-hour routine work of surveillance to a $200,000 industrial espionage case. While the average industrial investigation costs only $3,500, according to Milo Speriglio, president of the Los Angeles-based Nick Harris Detective Agency, more and more companies beset with increasingly complex problems such as congressional bribery hearings and Security and Exchange Commission investigations are looking for greater and more expensive expertise.

International Intelligence, Inc., or Intertel, for instance, is a large private detective agency run by Robert Peloquin, a former aide to Attorney General Robert F. Kennedy and the former head of the Federal Organized Crime Strike Task Force in Buffalo, New York.

"Mostly, we're a bunch of accountants," the publicity-shy Peloquin has admitted of his agency, which has offices across the country. It is true that Intertel is largely staffed with CPAs experienced in IRS audits and that corporations pay a minimum of $2,500 when hiring Peloquin, but considering the wealth of its clients and the unique experience of former government agents it hires, Intertel would be worth almost any price. It is not unusual for Intertel to have in its employ the same tax auditors and IRS investigators who may originally have worked on the client's tax fraud case or the same assistant United States attorneys who helped the government draw up the indictments Intertel's client is now trying to quash.

Like most private detective firms, Intertel is reluctant

to discuss its clients, but occasionally the company is identified when it is cited in court papers. Howard Hughes was among its clients, as were the owners of Paradise Island, the Bahamas gambling resort, who paid $350,000 a year to Intertel to keep organized crime figures from infiltrating their sunny paradise. The expertise, as well as the filing cabinets filled with organized crime names, which were acquired by Robert Peloquin while he was working for the government, can now be directed to the service of businessmen willing to pay the price.

The John T. Lynch Co., of Los Angeles, is another private detective agency made up of ex-federal agents and even a few retired CIA men. Lynch charges anywhere from $22 to $80 an hour and even boasts a special "Mission Impossible" team for major investigations. The minimum fee for that service is $15,000 and it includes attorneys, investigators, airplane pilots, and technicians skilled in electronic intelligence. It can even include a little theatrical makeup for the businessman who wants drama along with his investigations. The special appeal of Intertel and Lynch to the corporations that hire them, however, lies in the fact that these detective agencies are made up of some of the same attorneys and agents who earlier had helped prepare the cases for the government. Even if the agents did not work on the specific security fraud or antitrust cases at hand, they certainly are acquainted with some of the agents who did and are in a perfect position to know precisely how the federal cases against corporations are put together.

The ultimate prize for the hiring of federal agents,

however, must go to the International Business Machines Corporation, which simply hired itself an entire federal law enforcement agency. When IBM, a multinational company that is constantly on international guard against having its billion-dollar patents ripped off, hired John Ingersoll, the former head of the Federal Bureau of Narcotics and Dangerous Drugs, it hired the head of what had been one of the best informed and most widely scattered intelligence-gathering agencies in the world. When Ingersoll went over to IBM, he took along with him a great number of former agents and supervisors. Even Anthony Pohl, a former federal attorney who was generally regarded as *the* expert at constructing conspiracy cases, went along.

IBM not only hired the expertise of John Ingersoll and his staff, it also received the incalculable benefits that accrue from the friendship and camaraderie among narcotics agents, police chiefs, and intelligence agencies all over the world. Doors that would be firmly closed to an ordinary corporate cop are quietly opened for an honored, prestigious old friend. In addition, former heads of agencies invariably have access to domestic intelligence files. It's all unofficial, of course, but a former agency head usually has old and valued friendships within the bureau he once ruled, and, further, many of the G-men approaching retirement think of their ex-chief and his powerful spot in the private sector as a possible employer once they quit. All of these factors combined give former federal agency chiefs, such as John Ingersoll, extraordinary power as privately employed security men.

(*50*)

4 **F**or Irwin Blye, the game is different. He never was a federal agent. He was not a member of a law enforcement agency. He has no old partners in remote corners of the police bureaucracy to whom he can go for informative handouts. He knows hundreds of cops, detectives, federal agents, court clerks, probation officers, and prosecutors, but he is not a member of their club, and when Irwin Blye enters precinct houses and squad rooms, conversations usually stop. Blye is not a member of the law enforcement fraternity.

Nor, for that matter, is he a member in good standing of the fiction writers' private-eye establishment. He has very few of the characteristics we have come to expect of our private detectives from books, films, and television. Irwin Blye, for instance, is married. Aside from that supremely idealized marriage Dashiell Hammett concocted for Nick and Nora Charles, not one of the nation's invincible and fictional private detectives is married. Marlowe, Spade, Archer, Harper, Orwell, Hammer—none of them is married. They are not even engaged. They do not fret about their wives' birthdays or whether their children will be accepted at a private school. They do not have washing machines that back up sudsy messes in finished basements. They have no in-laws and are never required to appear at family functions or mow the lawn. The idea that Philip Marlowe might have to leave Geiger's house before the mystery of *The Big Sleep* is resolved in order to attend a birthday party would be enough of a shock to short-circuit every electric typewriter in Malibu.

In the real world of the private detective, where the exigencies of compact drama do not necessarily apply, mysteries are not solved at single encounters and truths do not emerge from sudden and cathartic revelations. Irwin Blye does not hang around his grubby office waiting for Lauren Bacall to show up in a cloud of jasmine with a $10,000 retainer. He does not keep a quart of Old Overholt in the bottom drawer of his desk. Blye does not even have drawers in his desk; what serves as a desk is a wobbly table lent to him by the law firm of Werner and Zaroff at 299 Broadway, in downtown Manhattan, from whom he rents a tiny room. Blye does not have an Effie of his own to relay messages and serve as straight man. A real Sam Spade, Blye must be content with a tape-

recorded answering service attached to his phone and
the kindnesses of secretaries employed by others. While
the 299 Broadway address is Blye's official, listed-in-the-
Yellow-Pages office, he also uses a tiny Queens Boulevard office across from the local courts.

Home to Irwin Blye is not a crummy furnished room
with a noisy iron bed and a neon sign that blinks outside
his window through the night. Blye, fiction fans will be
surprised to hear, lives in the suburbs. He has been married to the former Herta Holabeck for fourteen years.
They live in a tidy $65,000 red-brick-and-white-trim
house in a Long Island commuting suburb where all of
the winding streets and cul de sacs are named after trees
or American Indian tribes. The Blyes have an eleven-
year-old daughter, Elizabeth, who is in the fifth grade; a
six-year-old son, Anthony, who is in the first grade; a
one-year-old Irish setter named Taffy who is hyperactive;
a cramped one-car garage; and trouble with the septic
tank. Rather than lounge in waterfront bars at the end of
his working day, Irwin Blye goes home. During the day
and between surveillances and interrogations, Blye will
often catch a minute to call home and, as often as not,
be given a grocery list of items Herta might find difficult
to buy in their suburban Long Island shopping center.

"One of the advantages of Irwin's work," Herta explains, "is that he is likely to find himself just about
anywhere. If he says he's on the West Side, for instance,
I'll remember Zabar's has terrific Jamaican coffee beans
and ask him to pick some up. When he is in Brooklyn's
Flatbush there's a bakery we like."

When Irwin Blye backs his two-door, bronze-painted, three-year-old Matador out of the garage at eight-thirty every morning, he is indistinguishable from the hundreds of other commuting husbands on their way to work, except that Irwin Blye carries a .38 and does for a living what most of his neighbors have been watching on television the previous night. He makes about $50,000 a year, a little more than the average resident of his Colonial Park development, but he must work twelve to fourteen hours a day, six days a week, in order to keep his income at that level. He rises at six o'clock each morning, and while Herta hurries about the house assembling the children for school, Blye takes half a cup of coffee ("When you spend as much time as I do in cars on surveillance you learn to take in as few liquids as possible and to always have a wide-mouthed quart-sized jar in the car") to the basement where he usually spends an hour or two dictating very slowly into a $40 Panasonic tape recorder his detailed reports covering the cases he worked on the previous day. These reports include a letter to the attorney who employed him in the case and a careful reading of any signed statements he may have taken from potential witnesses. When Blye has departed for another day's sleuthing and Elizabeth and Anthony are in school, Herta spends a couple of hours transcribing in carbon triplicates everything Irwin had dictated into the tape recorder.

"She's really good," Irwin Blye acknowledges readily. "Herta has been doing this for so long that she sometimes spots holes in the investigation that I missed or forgot to plug. When I get home around nine or ten o'clock at night we usually go over the cases she typed that morning. If there is a particular problem she will tell the answering service that I should call home. Usually she doesn't have to do that, because I check in with the house two or three times a day."

When was the last time Mike Hammer called home?

Despite the gun and license to pry, Blye does not own a trench coat and his name certainly lacks the anvil clarity of a Spade, Harper, Marlowe, Hammer, Archer, clanged out on tough-talking typewriters. *Irwin Blye* is definitely not the kind of name that strikes terror in the hearts of felons. Also, Blye is not a very big man. He is, in fact, of medium size. At five feet eleven and 160 pounds, Blye cannot break through doors with his narrow shoulders, and despite the fact that he is quite strong as a result of a tough regimen of weight lifting and exercise, he has never intimidated people with his bulk.

"I know some former city detectives who are now PIs," Blye says, "who are so mean-looking and big that they just scare people into cooperating. I've seen them walk into offices and everyone from the receptionist to the boss wants to be their friend. It must be a tremendous help, but it's also got to be a crutch. When you've gone through life scaring people into giving you what they think you want, you're not going to get everything you need. It's too easy."

Blye has always had to depend on guile rather than brawn. It has made him a detective instead of just a gorilla and has far better prepared him for dealing with the increasingly complex computerized society with which today's private detectives must deal.

"You can't put the arm on a computer and scare it into giving you an alimony-ducking husband's address, but if you know the right code and can press the right buttons and know where the information is stored, that same computer can be made to cough up a nice little card with all the answers you need."

Even Blye's face falls far short of the fictional ideal. Dashiell Hammett began *The Maltese Falcon* with a description of his hero that rolls with satanic chilliness.

> Sam Spade's jaw was long and bony. His chin a jutting v under the more flexible v of his mouth. His nostrils curved back to make another, smaller v. His yellow-grey eyes were horizontal. The v *motif* was picked up again by thickish brows rising outward from twin creases above the hooked nose, and his pale brown hair grew down—from high flat temples —in a point on his forehead. He looked rather pleasantly like a blond satan.

In contrast, Irwin Blye is almost invisible. He disappears under examination. He looks as though he were drawn by freshmen art students who worked terribly hard at getting all of the parts of his face right, but forgot to sketch in any character. He has a round, bland, courteous face which is pleasant and instantly forgettable. His jaw, which neither juts nor recedes, is almost perfectly round and is punctuated right where it should be by a normal and totally undistinguished chin. His nose is long, straight, and thin, his nostrils flare slightly, but even these tender attempts at character are lost in the unrelieved pleasantness of his face. To go on too long about his face is to make more of it than there really is. Almond-shaped dark blue eyes, sharply etched smile creases, and neatly combed dark brown hair complete the picture. When he enters a room hardly anyone notices.

There are advantages, of course. Blye can follow an erring husband or wife for days, often standing right next to his subjects as they nervously await their lovers, and still they do not see him. He is the quintessential walk-on, one of the bland smiling people who serve as the background for the stars. Being a 42-year-old, five foot eleven, 160 pound white male drops Irwin Blye right into the middle of America's most statistically populous and anonymous mass. Rather than battle this anonymity, however, Irwin Blye, like Lamont Cranston, uses it to cloud men's minds.

To watch Irwin Blye at work is to see a man slowly disappear. Take your eyes from him for a moment and he is engulfed in a crowd. Blye does have props. His clothing, for instance, is chosen to blend with the day's assignment. He has what he thinks of as his FBI clothes (blue suit, white shirt, red tie), which he uses whenever he is interviewing the kinds of bureaucrats accustomed to talking to federal agents.

"It's that subliminal red, white, and blue," Blye says. "It makes lots of people want to stand up and salute."

There are several kinds of hats strewn about his car to persuade those being followed that they are not being followed. There are polyester resort clothes for sporty weekends in Miami Beach and the Caribbean, for lounging around the motel and hotel lobbies where much of his matrimonial work takes place. Blye even has the work clothes and well-scuffed construction workers' boots for those assignments on which any man in a suit and tie is immediately suspected of being a spy working for the boss.

More important than the props, however, is the experience of twenty years of tailing nervous people, taking statements from suspicious people, and gaining the confidence of violent people. According to Blye, experience is not just a matter of accumulating a sack full of tricks, but an intuition that dictates the right mode of action. Sometimes, though, even twenty years and intuition are not enough.

"Surveillance is probably the trickiest part of the business," Blye says. "I remember planting myself on the tail end of a Rolls-Royce I was watching for at least ten hours. It was a matrimonial case. He was rich. She was rich. She was planning to divorce him, but he found out and he secretly hired a lawyer and the lawyer hired me to see if she was doing anything that he could use. The husband didn't really care, he just wanted to be certain that she wouldn't be able to get any of his money in settlement. Fairly typical case, incidentally. Anyway, I'm on that Rolls-Royce all day long. She went from store to store, bank to art gallery, bakery to store. It went on for hours and finally the car pulled away from the curb and began going up Manhattan's West Side, the opposite side of town from where she lived, and pulled up in front of a Central Park West apartment house. For a minute I assumed that we had followed her to her rendezvous with romance, but then a man got out of the car and no one else. It was as though she had disappeared. Then I checked the license plate again and realized I had followed the wrong Rolls-Royce. I didn't even know how long I had been following the wrong car. No crisis. I just checked the day off as a loss and picked her up the next day. That time I didn't lose her or her Rolls-Royce.

"Car tails in the city are very tough. The traffic makes them almost impossible. Usually you need a couple of men. That way if the car's stuck, one guy can always jump out and continue to tail in a cab. Subways and buses are easier. You can lay back, stay further away from the subject. On buses in crowded areas, for instance, if I see my subject is about to get on a bus, I'll try to hotfoot it over to the next bus stop and get on there so that the subject will have no sense of me even being on the bus. Once I'm on, I go right to the back, the last row, where I can keep an eye on the back of the subject's head while he's looking out the window at the world.

"And sometimes you lose people. They just disappear on you. I once lost a two-hundred-twenty-pound woman in a yellow straw hat in Bloomingdale's. She wasn't even trying to lose me. She didn't know I was there, but somehow I lost her. It happens. Of course, it never happens to Cannon, but to real people like me it happens.

"On a surveillance the slightest distraction can be disastrous. If you miss someone coming out of a building you can spend the rest of the day watching a doorway for someone who will never appear. On surveillances, also, it often pays to have another person along. I usually hire one of about a half dozen guys who I use in situations where I need another witness to corroborate my testimony. When you have two guys working a surveillance, especially a long one, you can relieve each other once in a while. Otherwise you begin seeing things. I've been stuck alone on surveillances, looking at the entry to a house for as long as ten hours, and soon the doorway begins changing its shape and the pathway up to the door seems longer, or shorter, or crookeder, or anything different from what you thought it was just minutes earlier. You get to know these feelings after you've done lots of surveillance work. You learn to bite your lip, pinch your nose, anything to shake the mirage. I know detectives who have spent too many hours on plants and are ready to swear that they saw the Marx Brothers come dancing out of the office building they had under surveillance."

Besides knowing just about every trick in the trade, Blye also has an uncanny ability to be liked. Somehow he is able to mask the fact that he wants anything. He is polite and has a ready smile. He offers no threat to anyone. No matter whom Irwin Blye speaks to, there is no suspicion in his eye, no guile or connivance apparent in his visage. He is as pleasant and sympathetic with sadists in jail on Riker's Island as he is with their victims in hospital beds. It is an unnerving experience to watch him exude his balmy pleasantries indiscriminately.

"I want information. I want people to trust me. I don't want them to think I'm competing with them. I'm their audience. I clap. I smile. I laugh at bum jokes. I don't give a shit what they've done. As far as I'm concerned they were right. Nobody understands them. I do. I don't argue. I don't ask them why. Little by little I get close. Pretty soon I'm all they got.

"It's not just knowing how to talk to people. You've got to read them almost as you approach. People give off their personalities like perfume. They don't really have to say a word. Look at their clothes, what they do, the way they stand, how they seem to act to those around them, how they look at you, the light over their desk, the kind of things they've got around them. I can't really list all of the things that go into sizing up a person and figuring out how best to finesse a situation. On one occasion I spent four days in a midtown Manhattan bank rummaging through their records and questioning their employees in connection with an embezzlement case I was working on and only one bank official ever knew exactly who I was or what I was really doing there. I never lied to them. I just let them assume, and they assumed that I was the FBI."

Blye is extremely direct in presenting his credentials. He has the leather folding wallet in which he carries his private detective's license and his gun permit and he usually has the wallet open before he is close enough for the receptionist or secretary to read. Instead of closing his identification card upon reaching the person he wishes to bypass (as many private detectives pretending to be policemen do), Irwin Blye keeps his identification wallet open and practically shoves it under the eyes of the person he is approaching. He feels that people have a tendency not to read something too carefully when it is presented to them with such forthrightness.

In addition, the cards themselves have tended to confuse the average civilian to whom they are flashed. The three-by-five-inch laminated cards with a photograph of the bearer in the upper lefthand corner are usually kept in leather folding wallets with celluloid windows. The top of the card reads:

> State of New York
> DEPARTMENT OF STATE
> Division of Licensing Services

Under that official heading and totally obliterating the name of the bearer and the fact that he is a private investigator, there is an inch-and-a-half-wide seal of the state of New York. Then, at the very bottom of the card, out from under the seal, is the signature of the secretary of state and his title clearly printed in bold capital letters. The effect of the card and the way in which it is made up would give even the most wary and suspicious of people the impression that its bearer has some kind of official status. The card is simply a license from the state of New York, but it looks as though the bearer is actually an investigator for the state, rather than just another state licensee like a barber or an upholsterer.

"People see in the card what they expect to see," Blye says. "I've had businessmen read the card so carefully that I can see their lips move and they still think I'm with the FBI or the state troopers. When I tell people I'm a New York State-licensed private investigator, I can see them click me off at New York State. Incidentally, it doesn't matter how experienced people are in dealing with investigators.

"Banks, for instance, are always being bothered by cops and federal agents and tax men for one kind of information or another. That day I walked into that midtown bank I wanted to look and planned to act just like every pain-in-the-ass federal agent and auditor who ever walked in the door. I remember wearing my red, white, and blue G-man outfit. I was a walking flag. I remember that the manager's secretary hardly looked at my identification. She just assumed I was a federal agent or an auditor. I was courteous. I was filled with FBI 'thank yous' and 'excuse mes' and I was carrying my attaché case and I just knew how to hold it and how to stand.

"My job was to somehow get the bank to go through miles of their microfilm records to save my embezzler client's ass. Ha!

"I had no real plan, except that I knew if I told them I was a private detective representing an accused embezzler the chances of their going to a lot of trouble to help me were not very good. I couldn't go in and lie or pretend to be the feds because people go to jail doing things like that. What I had to do, what I always do, is plunge into the situation and play it by ear.

"There was something about the manager's secretary that I cannot explain, except to say that as I was approaching her desk I had this instinct that she was bored, that her boss was tough and officious, and that he ran a bank branch with lots of nervous people. I was right, it later turned out. The secretary sent me right back to her boss without really looking at my credentials at all.

" 'Pardon me,' I had said, 'I am a New York State . . .' but, typically, before I could even get it all out I knew she was gone in the head. She heard New York State licensed. . . . Who knows what she heard? I found out later that she had been yelled at by her boss for talking too much to various bank visitors, such as federal agents, and she was pissed. That's why she barely checked my ID. She was pissed and it was her manner that must have given her boss the impression that I was just another of an endless procession of nosy federal agents.

"When I approached him," Blye continues, "I had my license extended toward him in my official-looking black leather wallet. It is the same kind used by federal agents and cops. He hardly looked at my wallet. He was the kind of guy who wanted you to know he already knew who you were and what you wanted. And, that he was much too busy and important to be bothering with you. It's an attitude you run into all the time. It just exudes from certain guys.

"What he did, therefore, without really looking to see

who I was, and only half hearing what I wanted, was to call over his assistant manager in a tone like he was sending the guy out for coffee. He told his assistant that I needed help in connection with an embezzlement case and ordered the guy to help me. Little did he know I was on the embezzler's side. He told his guy to help me with anything I needed. The assistant manager, like all assistant managers, did everything he thought the manager wanted. And so for four days the poor guy went through spools of microfilm records for me. By the time I had what the embezzler's lawyer needed I was practically a fixture in that bank. I had my own desk and telephone. Tellers who I told who I was got me coffee and assumed their boss knew who I was too. The bank manager never knew who I was or what I was really doing in his bank. Neither did his assistant."

Irwin Blye does have one thing in common with his fictional colleagues. He carries a gun, a licensed .38-caliber Smith and Wesson. It is a tidy little metal-gray package. Blye wears it in either a special detective holster that fits snugly against his left hip or in a hanging shoulder holster that suspends the gun against the side of his chest, underneath his arm. The .38 does not have the stopping power of a .45, nor will it crash through an engine cylinder block like a .357 Magnum. It is a fairly accurate gun, however, and is the standard firearm used by the New York police. Although he visits a shooting range in Glen Cove once a month, Irwin Blye has never used his gun during business hours. In twenty years of participating in all kinds of capers, from murders to drug wars, Irwin Blye has never had to even draw his gun from its holster.

"I didn't have a gun for my first seven years," Blye says, "but my clients made me get one. I was doing a lot of matrimonial work at the time and I noticed that whenever I had a client they would always ask me whether or not I was armed. I would always say no and I could always tell that they were disappointed. Eventually the divorce lawyers I was working with at the time took me aside and explained that I owed it to my clients to get a gun.

" 'Look,' they said, 'they're paying for a private eye and even though you don't need a gun, the average client feels they want the detective they hire to at least have one.'

"It was a part of the theatrics of being a private detective," Blye goes on, "and theater is a major part of the job, especially in matrimonials. We're almost always brought in by the attorneys and paid by the clients and, for the most part, everyone involved is going through a very severe strain. During those times people are looking for strong lawyers and support. For lots of people, apparently, the gun helps. It's a prop. As far as I'm concerned that's all it is, even though it shoots real bullets and smells funny in the rain."

In real life, private detectives do not take out their guns every time they shove open the door of an empty house or apartment. Those scenes are almost a ritual in television and films. It is as if a private detective cannot get through a doorway without at least pulling his gun and then inching his way into the strange apartment.

According to Blye, private detectives do not go into strange apartments because, first, that is burglary, and, second, there are always dogs. Private detectives ring doorbells and talk to neighbors; they do not jimmy windows and slip in from fire escapes. If they think there might be something unusual going on in an apartment they will call the local police precinct and wait downstairs for the radio car to arrive. In fact, according to Blye, the frequency with which fictional private detectives use guns in their plots is absurd.

"Every time a television private eye goes in a door, or up a staircase, or does anything where he is the least bit uncertain, the first thing he does is pull out his gun. That's the pose. Gun in his right hand as he shoves open the unlocked door of the empty house or apartment. By the sound of the music you know he's going to find a body in there. And then if he sees anyone running from the building, or if he looks out an open window where the curtains are always blowing in the movie wind machine and sees somebody going down the fire escape, the private detective will give a couple of yells about stopping and then BAM! BAM! The guy turns around and he goes BAM! BAM! The detective BAM! BAM! The guy BAM! BAM! Nobody even knows what the hell has happened and they're BAM! BAMMING!

"What I've never seen in a movie or television is what happens to all those bullets. In the real world, let me tell you, every one of those goddam bullets is going to be accounted for by the police. I cannot emphasize strongly enough the police department's interest in discouraging gunfire among its own men and, most especially, among people who are licensed to carry guns but are not members of the department. The whole idea of the police department's licensing of private detectives to carry guns is exactly that. We're licensed to carry them, but absolutely never under almost any circumstances are we supposed to use the damn things.

"Once I was on a surveillance and I think a couple of guys might have been setting me up for a mugging, but when I opened my jacket and they saw my gun they just took off. That's not exactly *Gunfight at the OK Corral,* but that's the best story I got."

Irwin Blye is right. On a prime-time diet of shoot-'em-ups, it is almost impossible to believe that in 1974 in New York, for instance, only 599 policemen out of a force of 30,000 ever even fired their guns. Also, in New York, the city with eight million stories, Sin City, the crime capital where Charlie Bronson fulfilled everyone's death wish and Robert De Niro became everyone's taxi driver, in New York with all its organized crime and street gangs and drug wars, during an entire year there were only 740 incidents in which policemen fired their weapons. And those 740 incidents included everything from gun misfirings (15 per cent) to the shooting of hopelessly injured animals, mostly dogs (13 per cent).

In fiction, however, if the roscoe isn't barking out against crime in the night, its butt end is being indiscriminately used on people's heads. The private eye is close, about eleven minutes away from solving the crime, but he must be temporarily put out of action so that the rest of the plot can churn toward its conclusion without interference. What to do? Simple. Knock him out.

Scene: The detective, Alan Ladd, is seen walking through the darkened doorway of Claude Rains's mansion. Behind the door we have William Bendix holding a .45. As Alan Ladd approaches we pan to the butt of the gun held high and then we see the gun come crashing down on Alan Ladd's unsuspecting head. Quick cut to Bendix's face just before impact to show that Bendix meant business. FADE.

The room is dark. Outside we hear the dim honk of an errant horn. In the shifting light we can make out the supine figure of Alan Ladd. He is still. No. Wait a minute. He is moving. Yes, indeed. Alan Ladd is awake. His head moves. He begins to rise and then stops for a second. He is still very groggy. A pause. He reaches behind his head to feel where he was struck. He winces manfully. He begins to rise. He staggers a bit. He makes his way to the bathroom sink. (Private detectives who get hit in the head in strange houses all seem to know instinctively where the bathrooms are, even at Versailles.)

Alan Ladd turns on the tap. He hangs there a minute gathering strength. He splashes some water against his face. The music is no longer sonorous; in fact, all those minor chords slowly begin turning into major chords and they get louder. Within a minute or so Alan Ladd is back on the job. Bill Bendix, watch out. Damage? Forget it. Maybe a slight blemish on the right cheekbone, the kind that lovely, teary-eyed Gail Patrick was forever daubing with her tiny lace handkerchief.

"The scariest thing that I see on television and in the movies," Blye said, "is the casual way in which people are always hitting each other over the head. Kids watching that crap, even grownups, forget the effect of such blows. The television shows make it look as though getting hit over the head with a two-by-four has about the same permanent effect upon a person as two sleeping pills and a glass of warm milk. It's really crazy. And it's really dangerous.

"One shot like the kind those movie tough guys take week after week and you could be a vegetable for the rest of your life. I've had to spend long hours in hospital rooms trying to get the answers from people—sharp, young, tough people—who can no longer keep their thoughts together or the saliva inside their mouths after just one whack in the head from a cop's nightstick. I've seen people beaten up by kids who didn't know what a beating did to its victims. In some cases you talk to the kids and they have no concept of damaging people. It's as though they think everyone is going to show up in a week in the next installment. None of them can believe that just by hitting the guy in the head with the lead pipe that he'll never be able to see straight, that he'll have the kind of double vision that eyeglasses can't cure.

"It's not that everything they do in fiction is wrong or that being a private investigator is just like being an insurance agent. But the emphasis they portray is almost always wrong.

"Movie car chases are a good example," Blye continues. "Ever since *The French Connection* and *Bullitt* there

(70)

has been the usual car chase. The tires screech and everybody goes in every direction and one stunt is better than the next and it's like watching Demolition Derby. Great fun. But the point is that private detectives never chase anyone in a car. Hardly anyone ever chases anyone in a car. Highway cops chase speeders, sure. Radio-car cops chase guys after bank stickups, sure—once in a great while.

"This doesn't mean that private detectives don't go after people in cars; we do, but it's very very slow, not fast. In Hollywood the emphasis is on speed, but in reality the emphasis is in hanging on to your tail in the middle of midtown traffic, trying to stay close enough not to get trapped behind a light or truck, but not close enough to tip anyone off that they are being tailed. That kind of driving can be as exciting and crazy as any 110-mile-an-hour chase down 101. It's a matter of jockeying your car into position, anticipating what other cars in the traffic are going to do, and inching your way along without creating too much turmoil. In a traffic tail, for instance, sometimes you've got to quick change lanes and do the kinds of things that other drivers on their way home after a hard day think are crazy. Sometimes they let you know it. Nobody's going more than five miles an hour, so if somebody really gets mad at you they are likely to get out of their cars and start screaming in the middle of the traffic jam. That kind of thing attracts attention. It's not the kind of thing a really good private detective wants to do."

5 Monday. January 6, 1975.

It was going to be a fairly typical day in the life of private detective Irwin Blye. First, he would drive to his Queens Boulevard office and pick up a packet of material he had received from a South Carolina attorney representing Leo Timothy Berels, also known as Tiny, a three-hundred-pound carnival worker who had been accused of kidnapping a nineteen-year-old girl. Blye had spoken to the court-appointed lawyer, Robert Faucette, earlier in the week by phone and had been given an outline of what would be required of him in that case. The carnival worker had been arrested by the police of Dallas, North Carolina, where he lived, almost five months after the kidnapping took place. The Dallas police had happened on an old wanted circular for an unknown male, approximately Tiny Berels's weight and height, and decided to see if he might have been the culprit. The Dallas cops, who had had some barroom skirmishes with Tiny in the past, arrested him at the trailer camp on the outskirts of town where he lived with an attractive brunette widow and her two children. Tiny protested his innocence all the way to Spartanburg police headquarters, where the nineteen-year-old girl identified him as the man who had pressed the knife against her side and kidnapped her.

At his arraignment before the South Carolina federal district court Tiny Berels pleaded not guilty. He swore to everyone he spoke to that he was not guilty of kidnapping the girl. Since he was so poor that he could not raise any part of his $10,000 bail, the administrator of the federal district court assigned Tiny a local attorney, Robert Faucette. When Faucette first met with Tiny Berels, Berels insisted upon his innocence and said that he could prove he was not even in South Carolina at the time of the kidnapping. He said that he was employed by a carnival company at the time and was working in Lake Ronkonkoma, on Long Island, New York. Tiny Berels began telling Bob Faucette about the places he lived and drank and the names of the carnival companies for whom he worked. Any one of them, Tiny Berels insisted, could prove that he was in New York.

Enter the private detective. Tiny had, of course, told the FBI and the local police the same story, but as they already had a girl positively identifying him as her kidnapper, their hearts were not in finding out that their principal witness might have been mistaken. The FBI had checked with the carnival owners, but since Tiny had been paid in cash and his Social Security benefits and taxes had not been paid by the owners, they told the FBI that they were not sure on which of three days Tiny Berels was last employed by them. The three days they decided upon, according to the FBI, were either the day before the kidnapping, the day of the kidnapping, or the day after the kidnapping. Neither the FBI nor the local police who arrested Tiny bothered to check out any of the other people he claimed could prove that he was in New York at the time of the kidnapping. This is not an unusual police attitude. If the man they arrested says he has an alibi, the general feeling among cops is that it is pretty much the responsibility of the man arrested to prove his innocence.

Thus, attorneys representing clients charged by the police with various crimes find it difficult to accept the police version of what happened. They also cannot believe that the cops did everything in their power to check out all of the defendant's alibis. In order to make the necessary inquiries, therefore, attorneys need the services of private investigators. It is the private detective who is charged with checking out all of the facts, all of their client's alibis, all of those witnesses who might contradict the witnesses called by the police. In the preparation of his case and through a number of pretrial motions, the defense attorney has tremendous legal powers. He can subpoena all kinds of bank records, em-

ployment sheets, sales slips, personal diaries—anything
he thinks might convince the judge—whatever is necessary for him to be able to present an adequate defense.
It is usually the private investigator who advises the attorney on potentially fruitful items to subpoena and it
usually takes a court order before most businesses and
banks will bother to dredge up the necessary papers,
even if it is a matter of life and death.

Good private detectives are rare. The same names are
mentioned over and over whenever defense attorneys
are looking for the kind of investigators who will do more
than just rewrite police reports. It didn't take Robert
Faucette long to come up with the name of Irwin Blye.
Since the federal court will allow only $15 an hour for the
services of a private investigator, with the fee never to
exceed $250, Faucette had to find a private detective who
worked in the area where most of the inquiries would be
made. To fly a local man up to New York would have
used up most of the defense attorney's investigation
fees, so Bob Faucette relied upon the advice of some
local attorneys and gave Irwin Blye a call.

After talking with Faucette, Blye made a few telephone
calls of his own. First he checked to make sure that the
carnival company Tiny had said he worked for actually
existed. It did, but the carnival owner, Harry Fried, was
not there. Time enough. Blye would check out the name
of the bar Tiny had said he frequented during the month
of June when he was working in the New York carnival.
A few more telephone calls and a trip out to Lake Ronkonkoma to get signed statements from any of the wit-

nesses who could swear that Tiny was with them in New York on the day he was supposed to have kidnapped a girl in Spartanburg and Irwin Blye would have earned his $250.

The best witnesses, of course, would have to be flown down to the trial at the court's expense and it would be up to Blye to help Bob Faucette decide which of the witnesses would be most useful in front of a South Carolina jury. This is one of the reasons Blye includes in all of his reports physical descriptions of the people he talks to and takes statements from. He will describe them as well mannered, or pleasant-faced, or seemingly forthright. He will also warn attorneys away from potential witnesses whom he considers poor risks, witnesses who may have criminal records or personality quirks that might annoy a jury.

"Some witnesses just look and sound like they're lying, even when they're telling the truth," Blye says. "And others are just the opposite. I'll take the latter, anytime."

On this cold and wintry morning in January, Blye planned to drive out to the bar and carnival hangouts on Long Island where Tiny Berels said his friends could be found. Blye would take statements corroborating Tiny's claims and size up the best, or most convincing, of Tiny's potential witnesses.

Next, Blye would turn the car around and head for upper-income Hartsdale where he would have to listen to the property settlement battle plans of an outraged doctor's wife. She had been separated from her husband for about a year and a half, and while it had started amicably, he had recently begun canceling her department store charge accounts. The doctor's wife felt he had also been slowly siphoning money out of their joint accounts. She suspected that after twenty years of marriage and three children grown, he was getting ready to dump her.

Before he could do that, she wanted to make sure he was not hiding any of the assets that they had accumulated as a couple. She did not want her husband to go into court at settlement time and be able to pretend he was poorer than she knew he was. She wanted to hire Irwin Blye to find out exactly how much money and property her husband really had, not how much he was telling the tax people.

The last thing on Blye's schedule for the day was a trip to the South Bronx where he had an appointment to talk with a fifty-five-year-old woman who had been scalded over 60 per cent of her body because the city had failed to fix her hot water faucet. This one was a straight bread-and-butter negligence case. A knowlegeable lawyer had learned of the woman's situation and realized that her injuries were probably worth $65,000. The woman, who was on welfare, had been regular with her rent and had repeatedly complained to the superintendent that the hot water valve in her bathroom was broken. Since the accident, the city had taken over the building. She had complained to the city, and since the city could not sneak out on its responsibility as most landlords could, and since the woman had been seriously injured and there was a police department report on her injury as well as a two-month-long record from the hospital where she had been under intensive care, culpability and proof of injury were assured. All the lawyer wanted from Blye was a statement from the woman and a statement from her daughters who could attest to the condition of the faucet and a statement from the superintendent that she had asked him to fix the faucet and that he had been unable to. Blye would get $150 from the lawyer for the South Bronx job and $200 in advance from the Hartsdale housewife, as well as the $250 for tracking down Tiny-the-carnival-worker's pals. Blye felt the morning had the makings of a very good day.

Real private detectives, like Irwin Blye, do not have the luxury of working on one case at a time. Blye could not afford to chase after Brigid O'Shaughnessy and the Maltese Falcon for a week and let the rest of his clients wait. On any one day, Irwin Blye might work on as many as a dozen cases. Between the interviews with potential witnesses and motel vigils there are hours spent in telephone booths trying to pick up the odd bits and pieces of people's lives. His office is wherever he happens to be.

Swirling around on the back seat of Blye's dusty Matador that January morning was the paperwork relating to the three or four dozen other cases with which he was also concerned. There were letters from lawyers, slips of paper with docket numbers, court depositions, Xeroxed transcripts of dubious testimony, expense vouchers that had not been paid, Dun and Bradstreet statements, accident reports, pads of government forms for requesting information, sheets of ruled paper on which to take witnesses' statements, and sarcastic notes to lawyers who are always welching on his fees.

Among the papers was a request from lawyers for an art gallery who wanted to find the daughter of an old-time movie star. Using her father's name she had taken a painting on consignment and had not returned it when requested to. She had moved from the address she had given, a crummy hotel. And when it was learned that she made a living as a stripper and go-go dancer, the gallery's lawyers decided to hire Blye to find the girl and get back the painting.

There was the case of Lucy Best, whose husband was looking for a reduction in alimony and child support payments because he claimed he was now only a salesman for a Syracuse, New York, photography supply company. Mrs. Best was certain that he had bought the company and was only pretending to be a salesman in order to get his support payments reduced. Blye was going to have to fly to Rochester later in the week and check out the woman's intuition. He guessed she was probably right. Wives are almost always right when it comes to psyching out their husbands.

There were other cases, too. One was a homicide involving a Manhattan woman who was charged with having her husband killed by a bartender lover so she could use the insurance money to open a night club. The newspapers played that story up quite a bit, but none of them realized that the murder took place not over the insurance money, but over a cocaine ring her husband had been heading. The cops had put so much pressure on the bartender that he and a friend of the woman confessed that the woman planned the murder, and that, in fact, she had hired them to commit the murder. Blye had been all over town trying to dig up dirt to besmirch the character of the police's bartender-witness, but Blye doubted if that alone would be enough to save the woman.

Blye was also working for two women who had just bought a building off Times Square that they planned to convert into a luxury massage parlor with saunas, steam rooms, and swimming pool. The building had originally housed a health club and the two women, both of whom had been arrested for prostitution in the past and had run massage parlors throughout the city, said they were being harassed by city officials who had their own personal designs on the building. The women told Blye that city officials, hoods, and real estate lawyers had been surprised when it became known that two women had bought the valuable site. Blye was hired to prove that there was a conspiracy on the part of the city officials and the hoods to deny the women the use of their own building. They had given Blye the names of women who managed midtown massage parlors who would tell him about the plot. They also gave him the name of a Brooklyn court official who could give him all the background of the case. Blye had the impression that the Brooklyn court official was a silent partner with the two women in the deal.

There were other cases, as well. Blye had as a client a Connecticut psychiatrist in her early sixties who said that she had been seeing a gentleman for about two years and had grown very dependent upon him. The only problem, the psychiatrist told Blye, was that the man was extraordinarily secretive and mysterious. He refused to give her his home address and telephone number. He refused to say what he did, except to say that he worked for the federal government and that much of his work was top secret.

"How did you meet him?" Blye had asked.

"I had gone downstairs to a luncheonette in my office building and he sat next to me and we struck up a conversation," the psychiatrist said. "He was very nice and we met there on other occasions."

"Did you sit next to him or did he sit next to you?"

"He sat next to me," the psychiatrist said.

"Was the place crowded?"

"No," she answered, "I always take my break after the busy lunch hour."

"How long have you been seeing him and how often?"

"He comes to my home on Tuesdays and Thursdays around one o'clock in the afternoon and leaves at about five o'clock."

"Do you go out anywhere?"

"No."

"When you do go out, where do you go?"

"We've only gone out once."

"Once in two years?"

"Yes."

The man had said he was separated from his wife and family and lived in New York. He claimed that his support payments strapped him considerably and that his super-secret government job did not really pay him enough for him to drive up to Connecticut two days a week for their dates. After a few weeks, the psychiatrist told Blye, she began giving the man $150 a week in order for him to rent a car and drive up to see her.

What the psychiatrist wanted Blye to do was verify the identity of her gentleman friend. She wanted to know everything about him, where he lived, what he really did, everything. At the same time, however, the psychiatrist tried to rationalize everything Blye said that might be construed as a criticism of her friend.

"She said that she didn't want to destroy her relationship with him if any part of the story he had been telling her is true," says Blye. "It was amazing to listen to someone as smart as that woman being so gullible about a guy who was obviously a con man setting her up for a touch."

The cases pile up and private detectives like Blye move from one to the other day after day, picking up a piece of one case on Tuesday, another fact on Thursday and, if they're lucky, perhaps the final piece to the puzzle on the weekend. No time is wasted. Even weekends with the family are used. For instance, some real estate lawyers recently hired Blye to find a former partner who had moved from his address several years ago and whom no one had been able to find. Blye found the man's new address by going to the post office that covered the area of his old address and paying a postal clerk $5 to dig up one of the old "removal books." Post office removal books, or change-of-address books, are usually kept for about a year, but for $5 most clerks will search through the dusty bins long enough to find back issues. Blye found the man's new address in a two-year-old book and planned to double-check by visiting the area over the weekend with his wife, Herta, and the children.

"House-hunting is a terrific way to knock on people's doors," Blye says. "You pretend you got the addresses screwed up, but getting the new directions usually gives you enough time to judge whether the people who live there fit the description of the people you've been asked to find.

"And with a blonde wife and two kids waiting in a car at the curb, even the wariest types fail to become suspicious."

There was also the Brooklyn case of the sixteen-year-old girl who had regressed into childhood after having gone out on a date with a U.S. Army recruit from the neighborhood. The girl's mother was paying Blye $500 to find out what the soldier had done to her daughter, but Blye was not yet certain that the girl had actually regressed. He was also suspicious of the girl's mother. The woman lived on the third floor of a Flatbush Avenue shoestore in a filthy apartment with four snarling and barking dogs. The woman was separated from her husband, lived on welfare, and was dominated by the sixteen-year-old boyfriend of one of her other daughters. She paid Blye to find out about her daughter, but he did not know where she got the money. The mother had told him she had a dear friend who was rich and gave her all the money she needed. Blye knew he was going to have to go back to that kennel where the woman and her daughters lived later in the week.

Flapping away somewhere on Blye's back seat was a request from a Madison Avenue advertising man who planned to divorce his wife and wanted to be sure that she did not try to take him for everything he owned. His lawyer, a matrimonial "bomber" for whom Blye often worked, had suggested that the advertising man hire a private detective to see if his wife, from whom he was then only separated, might have a lover. The adman had resisted but the lawyer had insisted. Blye planned to get around to talking with the adman later in the week.

There were other cases. There were negligence cases and missing persons and a homosexual suicide involving the bathtub slaying of somebody's mother and stolen antiques. Jammed into manila envelopes and folders in the back seat of Blye's car were scores of bizarre dramas with which he would eventually have to deal. After twenty years they were almost routine to him, but not quite. His pace still quickened as he started off for work in the morning. There were many men who made more money than he and there were certainly those who did not have to spend the interminable hours he spent making it, but there was nothing in the world that Irwin Blye would rather have done.

6 I was leaning against the bar in a speakeasy on Fifty-second Street, waiting for Nora to finish her Christmas shopping, when a girl got up from the table where she had been sitting with three other people and came over to me. She was small and blonde, and whether you looked at her face or at her body in powder-blue sports clothes, the result was satisfactory. "Aren't you Nick Charles?" she asked.

I said: "Yes."

The Thin Man by DASHIELL HAMMETT

Not quite Irwin Blye's milieu. Irwin does not wait for Herta at 21 and he doesn't work his cases out of a suite of rooms in the Normandie. In fact, if one were to find

Irwin Blye hanging around anywhere in New York it would probably be at the Silver brothers' Carl & Leon luncheonette in Rego Park, Queens.

"Never eat anything there that isn't wrapped in the factory," Blye insists, "but the action is terrific. The Silvers, I suspect, run one of the city's great swag centers. Stolen goods. You can walk in there on one day and get a fur coat for your wife and on the next day they're pushing typewriters. Carl Silver will notarize legal papers, even though he's not a real notary. He just got hold of a notary stamp somewhere and he's been notarizing ever since. He even did a $100,000 will recently. He's the ultimate white collar crook. For instance, he never pays for the food he sells. Milk. Eggs. Danish. Coffee. Everybody waits forever to get paid and then he'll only pay off a few cents on the dollar. He's been to court so often that I've seen him selling jewelry to court clerks. He owes the government $56,000 in back taxes, sells cars from the parking lot in the rear of the store, has an enamel business that touches up chips in bathtubs and sinks damaged during construction, and he runs a roofing business in Florida from a pay phone in the rear of the luncheonette. He gets calls all day long from sucker contractors looking for roofing materials and as soon as he hangs up on one guy he calls some other guy and makes the deal, taking his middleman percentage, of course.

"He just stands there," Blye continues, "leaning against the phone in the rear of the store in his dirty apron with a spatula in his hand, fighting off school kids who want to use the phone and putting together roofing deals in Tampa."

Silvers' luncheonette is long, narrow and crowded. On one side there is a marble counter at least twenty-five feet long with twelve cushioned stools that are spun noisily by the youngsters who frequent the place. There are also six caramel-colored hard maple wood booths that line the opposite wall, but they are filled with bookkeeping paraphernalia, adding machines, rolled-up blueprints, brochures announcing new Silver ventures, and an assortment of Silver pals and cronies engaged in symbiotic enterprises. There are bookmakers, loan sharks, fences, shoe salesmen, cabbies, retired cops, and their hustling buddies from the local precinct shuffling in and out of the Silver booths all day long.

The heart of Silvers' luncheonette, however, is not Carl Silver's phone-booth magic, but the cash register bunker in which his brother, Leon Silver, is said to live. Customers can hardly see Leon. He is immersed in newspapers, magazines, candies, plastic combs, cigarette cartons, tout sheets, numerology books for numbers players, cigar boxes, chewing gum, pocket handkerchiefs, Alka Seltzer packets, aspirin tins, rolls of stomach tablets, wooden pencils, ball-point pens, and lottery tickets. From behind his festooned window Leon's arm shoots out snatching money from the hands of his customers and almost instantaneously returning them their change. Leon doesn't come out from behind the register and talk to people even when business is slow, when

customers aren't lined up in front of his little opening.
Leon stays at his post. On rainy afternoons he can be
seen seated on a high stool watching a four-inch television set he has plugged into his tiny cubicle. He also has
a transistor radio, stacks of half-read newspaper and
magazine articles, and a shelf filled with paper containers
of half-drunk tea.

"I enjoy the place," Blye says, "and since it's within
walking distance of my unofficial Queens office I prefer
meeting people there, over a cup of coffee, than in a
stuffy room."

Even Blye's unofficial Queens office is the office of a
man who hates offices. It is on the second floor of a
grubby two-story cinder-block and casement-windowed
building on Queens Boulevard, across the street from
the County Courts. On the ground floor is a topless
restaurant, a couple of bail bondsmen, a travel agency
that specializes in traveler's checks and tours of the
quickie divorce islands, and some tax consultants
jammed desk-to-desk in a tiny storefront that was once
a shoeshine parlor. The building's lobby was painted an
institutional gray many years ago. Instead of a rug or
carpeting, a strip of black rubber matting runs between
the front door and the tiny elevator that inches its way
between the basement and second floor, balking when
more than four people wedge themselves inside. The
second floor of the building has the same gray walls, but
here the floors are covered with maroon and black lino-
leum squares. There are at least a dozen law offices and
even at eight o'clock in the morning there are clusters of

men whispering into each other's ears and elbowing their way past with a briskness that borders on rudeness. No one, however, seems to mind. It is as though the adversary system of justice had been extended to the streets and offices and it is unthinkable for one attorney to hold a door for another or not rush past a third in a flurry of elbows and knees in order to get a spot on the tiny elevator.

Blye does not have his name on the door of his office. In fact, the office in which Irwin Blye has his office isn't really his office at all. He sublets a small room in the law offices of Salaway and Schrieber, a Queens Boulevard firm made up of ambitious young, city-bred attorneys who specialize in real estate, criminal, negligence, matrimonial, corporate, and tax law. Blye pays Salaway and Schrieber $75 a month for a nine-by-nine-foot room with a door that he cannot close. (The wooden door has no doorknob and there is a hole where the lock cylinder should be.) There are two chin-high metal file cabinets in two of the room's corners and they, like the desk, bookshelves, and chairs, are piled high with a jumble of legal papers, lined yellow pads, old coffee containers filled with the curled and blackened ends of cigarettes, week-old newspapers, law books, legal briefs, reference books for checking telephone numbers and home addresses, affidavits, and a wide variety of requisition forms with which Blye is able to wheedle information out of the bureaucracy. One blackened window hides the smoke and grease ducts from the go-go restaurant below. A huge, dusty air conditioner rests on the windowsill. On top of it are a staple machine with no staples, more old coffee containers, and a stack of spiral, pocket-size notebooks. On the corner of Blye's cluttered desk is a small college-model electric portable on which he occasionally pecks out dunning letters to various attorneys who have been slow to come across with the money they owe him.

Many of the buildings around New York's courts cater to the hustlers of the criminal justice system. There are notary publics, bail bondsmen, defense attorneys specializing in arson, others specializing in organized crime. There are process servers who lie about service, there are former state legislators and city councilmen looking for cozy middleman roles between troubled businessmen and city and state officials looking for bribes. There are labor relations advisors who are little more than old-fashioned extortionists, guaranteeing labor peace in return for monthly retainers. There are also former judges (one of whom was forced off the bench for an ambulance-chasing scheme, and another as a result of a noisy paternity suit) who now serve as attorneys for landlords, the liquor lobby, nursing home investors, and anyone looking for a little extra in their suits.

In this world, bribery is a way of life. Legislators lobby for bills that favor businesses they own through dummy corporations with money they received under the table to fight against the same bills. The triple-cross is commonplace. Even the men entrusted with the maintenance of honesty and decorum in government are a part of the same frazzled system. For instance, there is a commission made up of politically appointed lawyers who sit in judgment on private investigators who have, in one way or another, found themselves the subjects of complaints. This Private Investigators Advisory Committee is made up of about a dozen members appointed by the secretary of state, New York's major licensing official, who oversees every state-licensed business from billiard parlors and barbershops to steamship ticket agents and upholsterers. It is a massive boondoggle for backscratching pols. The lawyers who appear before various committees representing clients in need of licenses of one sort or another have often served as committee members themselves.

A long-time committee member was an attorney named Sylvester Garamella. He passed on new applications and he also sat in judgment on private investigators who were charged with violating state rules. Garamella, a Republican, had been appointed during the administration of Governor Nelson Rockefeller. Garamella was also identified as a one-time partner in the Manhattan-based labor relations firm of S.G.S., where his two partners were Henry H. Saltzstein, a convicted burglar and bookmaker, and George Schiller. In April of 1955 the firm of Saltzstein, Garamella, and Schiller, S.G.S., was changed slightly when Garamella quietly withdrew from the company and his "G" initial was taken by the late crime boss of bosses, Carlo Gambino. Gambino remained a partner in the firm for approximately ten years.

S.G.S. had many clients, including Wellington Associates, a major realty firm that owned, among other properties, the Chrysler Building. William J. Levitt, whose suburban developments carry his name and were built largely without union labor, used S.G.S. as a labor consultant. S.G.S. has found labor peace for hospitals, resort hotels, clothing manufacturers, and retailers. Even after *New York Times* investigative reporter Charles Grutzner exposed the Garamella connection with S.G.S., Garamella retained his state post. It was not, in fact, until 1976 that Garamella left the Private Investigators Advisory Committee. He now practices law and specializes in representing private investigators who appear before the same advisory committee on which he once sat.

Within law enforcement circles, one of the reasons that private investigators have often been held in such low esteem is that some of them are regularly employed by organized crime figures. A private detective is licensed to carry a gun and he is essentially a gun for hire. Many of them, especially former police officers and detectives who may have been forced out of their jobs because of corruption, apply for private investigators' licenses and then go to work for some of the same racketeers from whom they had taken money when they were cops. Vincent Papa, for instance, one of the world's major narcotics dealers, has long employed as a bodyguard a private investigator who was a New York City narcotics detective. The two men have traveled the world together and the dealer is never far from his absolutely legitimate and well-armed bodyguard. Papa is not the only organized crime heavy who has hired licensed protection. Crooks have come a long way since the days when they hired local gorillas with unregistered guns. Police esti-

mate that there are dozens of licensed private investigators, most of them former cops, currently in the employ
of racketeers and drug pushers.

"These guys not only protect those bums from other
bums who want to shoot them," a federal prosecutor in
the narcotics field says, "but they give away secrets, try
to find out about our witnesses, and have even served as
killers when paid to do so."

In this world but not of it, Blye thinks of himself as a
specialist. His is a business of specialized knowledge.
Where many of his contemporaries are baffled by the
intricacies of the bureaucracy, Irwin Blye has learned to
thread his way through the Kafkaesque wilderness of the
computer and emerge with answers. He has profited
from his ability to manipulate red tape.

According to Irwin Blye, information equals power. It
does not matter that he cannot crash through doors and
that he is not an ex-cop or FBI man with semiofficial
access to official records. His particular genius lies in his
ability to deal with the vast American bureaucracy itself.
Where most Americans are baffled by the impersonal
layers of red tape and irrational delays that afflict them,
Irwin Blye has learned to manipulate them. He has used
the spindle-free apparatus for his own ends and turned
the bureaucracy against itself. He is the master of paperwork, the Napoleon of triplicate, the ultimate manipula-
tor of the written request. Blye understands that the
myriad offices of governmental administrations hold the
answers to all questions. The key lies in knowing precisely how to trigger that great impersonal machine into

coughing up the right juicy tidbits. Blye has made the corridors of government his own.

"Here, see this form?" Blye says, waving a letter-size sheet of paper. "It's an M.V. 198 G. It's issued by the Motor Vehicle Bureau, and anyone who wants one can get it. It is a simple request for a copy of a driver's license. It's what you would use if you lost your own license. With a minimum amount of information and a $3.50 fee I can find out more about people from this one piece of paper than they would ever imagine.

"I remember one woman who said she had been looking for an illegitimate son for twenty years. Her parents had convinced her to give the baby to a couple who were living in Yonkers at the time. But after a few days without her baby she went to the Yonkers apartment to ask for her baby back, but the couple were gone. She had been looking for her baby ever since and, according to her lawyer, the search had cost her several thousand dollars.

"I told her that I couldn't guarantee anything, but I asked her for her son's date of birth, the name she had given the boy, the name the couple had called him, her last name, and the last name of the couple to whom she had given the child. With that information I filed two different M.V. 198 Gs, one requesting a copy of a driver's license for a man with the last name and date of birth of the child and one using the last name of the couple who raised him. As long as you've got an exact date of birth and a name, the Motor Vehicle Bureau's computer can come up with the license. Within a month I was sent a copy of the guy's license. He was using the last name of the couple and the address where he was living was right there on a copy of his driver's license.

"When I told the woman I had found her son she let out such a scream I got scared. I thought she was a nut. I wouldn't give her the address until she calmed down and said that she realized he might not even know that she existed. She said that all she wanted was to see that he was okay. She was going to drive out to where he lived and just look at him.

"Aside from filling in an address for someone you're looking for, the M.V. 198 G also gives you a man's height, weight, and color of his eyes. If he has a chauffeur's license you even get his picture. That same form can be used to find out if a driver has had his license suspended, or revoked. It will also tell me whether the person drives with eyeglasses, needs a hearing device, is crippled in any way and needs special controls, and whether or not the subject ever got tickets for speeding."

7

Even without the powers of subpoena, the legitimate sources of personal information about clients and subjects available to private detectives such as Irwin Blye are a civil libertarian's nightmare. The Motor Vehicle Bureau, according to Blye, is one of his favorite sources.

"At some point in an investigation somebody always uses a car and they invariably meet somebody else who uses a car," Blye says. "If a subject stays home and we have the house under surveillance, guests are always driving up in automobiles, visiting for a while and then driving away. The Motor Vehicle Bureau will not only tell you who the cars belong to, but will describe the owner and tell you just about everything you want to know about him or her."

When Blye wants to know to whom an automobile belongs he usually finds out by either sending $2 to the Motor Vehicle Bureau with an M.V. 15 registration information request form upon which he has filled in the car's license plate number, its year, and its make, or paying a record service company in Albany to get it for him. Within days he gets a reply listing the name of the car's owner, his address, his driver's license number, and the date of his birth. Most private detectives charge their clients anywhere from $10 to $25 for finding the owner of a car. Many of them pretend that they have to pay off detectives in order to get that kind of information. Lawyers go along with the charade, knowing that it is a way that the privates supplement their income.

By requesting a copy of applications filed for drivers' licenses, Blye can also find out whether the driver has a heart condition, a record of mental illness, whether he has ever been confined to a public or private institution or hospital, and whether he has ever received treatment for alcoholism or narcotics addiction. Using his cartons of forms and an endless supply of envelopes and stamps, Blye can find out whether the driver has ever been arrested, where he is currently employed, and how long he has been there. In other words, he uses the Motor Vehicle Bureau as the basis for a great many background investigations and, depending upon what he wants and what he finds, he decides whether or not to continue his inquiries.

"As far as I'm concerned," Blye says, "the world's greatest source of information is not some crummy guy who waits for you outside a Bowery bar, but a gentleman by the name of Julius Blumberg. Without him there's no way any private detective could get enough information to make a living. Julius Blumberg is the largest printer of legal forms in the world. You can get a legal form requesting any kind of available information from Julius. When I was just beginning I used to spend hours at his office at 80 Exchange Place poring over the kinds of things that were available through Julius. I found one little item, for instance, that has been a tremendous help to me. Its official title is Copy-Form UCC-11, but what it does is tell you everything you want to know about anyone who has ever applied for a loan or has ever had a lien placed against him anywhere in New York State. The UCC-11 is part of the Uniform Commercial Code law, which requires all loans and liens to be filed with the county clerk's office. Banks, finance companies, everybody who lends money in the state except the loan sharks forward the information you turn over to them when you apply for a loan to the county clerk. Then I come along with Julius Blumberg's UCC-11 and a $3 fee to the same county clerk and within a couple of weeks I've got all of your little financial secrets.

"For instance, all I ask for my $3 fee is whether or not Ray Monte, of 123 Tent Walk, Brooklyn, has any judgments against him. What I get back is the following:

Blye, Private Eye

General Electric Credit Corp.—26 Court St. Bklyn.
VS
Ray Monte—146 Jamaica Avenue, Jamaica, N.Y.

(Now I know little Ray has another address)

Joseph Coste, 282 Grand Blvd., Woodmere, N.Y.

(Now I know the name of an associate to whom he owes money, and just maybe that old associate is not such a pal.)

> *Index No. 15436-75 Year—'75*
> *Amount: $392.33*
> *Court: Civil-Kings*
> *Docket: 11-18-75 Perfected: 5-1-75*
> *Attorney: Jack Taube, 26 Court St., Bklyn.*

"Depending upon the importance of the case there are any number of threads that I could pick up on. There is the Joe Coste angle, and there is the lawyer who might know something of a nonconfidential nature that he could pass along, and then there is the guy's different address and Coste's address. America is information-happy and the only trick is in knowing what you want and where to find it. There are even shortcuts. For instance, there is a huge abstract index system in New York at 85 John Street. For a modest fee all you have to do is type in the name and address and age of whoever you want and, whammo, out comes a three-by-five index card that lists any time that person's name has ever appeared on an official report. It's scary. Here's a card that shows that a woman, Beverly Green of 3917 14th Avenue, Brooklyn, thirty-six, female, married, had an accident on 3-19-74 at 10th Avenue, near 48th Street, Brooklyn, and that she was taken to Maimonides Hospital with a bruised right knee where she was treated by Dr. Strout, of Maimonides, and released. She later had a miscarriage and filed a claim against the hospital, using as her attorney Daniel Cardone, of 123-60 83rd Avenue, Kew Gardens. The card also shows that she was insured by the Federation of Jewish Philanthropies and the Travelers Insurance Company of 80 John Street.

"Is there any doubt in your mind as to how many threads one could pick up from just two little three-by-five index cards supplied for a couple of bucks by the New York Index Bureau? It's amazing, however, because in doing background investigations on various people, even professionals such as lawyers and other privates don't know about or use all of the little bureaucratic nooks and crannies of our red tape society. Insurance company investigators and credit company people are almost always helpful. I can call some finance companies, for instance, and they'll usually read me the subject's loan application and on that, of course, the subject has to list his earnings, the names of his relatives, where he banks. I can also find out if the subject has any judgment against him by simply going to the county clerk's office where the subject resides. There, in alphabetical order,

I can look for the subject's name. If he does have a judgment outstanding against him, then I call the company listed in the clerk's office and get a copy of the judgment and a wealth of other information about the subject. If I'm too busy I'll sometimes write to the Record Abstract Corporation at 186 Joralemon Street in Brooklyn and send them a $7.50 check and let them make the credit search for me.

"Using these information-gathering offices and using hundreds of Julius Blumberg's different forms you can find out just about anything you want to know about anyone. The irony is that if you go to the wrong people for that information, you'd get the impression that there was no way possible that you could get to know what you want to know. I know collection agency people who used to pay cops hundreds of dollars a month just to check license plates for them. The department cracked down on the practice and some guys lost their jobs and some privates lost their licenses.

"A town's tax collector is another great source of information. If I'm trying to find someone who I know lives on Long Island, for instance, and he has an unlisted phone or a phone under someone else's name, I can always check to see if the person I'm looking for is paying a water bill. In suburban communities, everybody pays a water bill and while somebody might use a different name for his telephone listing, taxes are another matter. All I have to do is give the tax collector the name of the person I'm looking for and he gives me the address. Besides water taxes, of course, there are school taxes, city, village, and county taxes, a whole range of taxes where tax collectors have information that is available to the public either for free or for a $2 fee.

"It's all so simple, yet clients and their lawyers are all so sure that I'm getting that information in some kind of illegal manner. Usually they feel that I have some contact in the telephone company who slips me unlisted telephone numbers and addresses. No point in telling them I often get the numbers and addresses from a county clerk off a water bill or a school tax form. They'd never want to pay the $75 to $125 fees for such information.

"There's an invaluable book that I use. It is called *Cole's Metropolitan Householders Directory,* and it is a telephone book that must have been made in private detective heaven. It's put out by an independent company, at 485 Lexington Avenue, and I suspect it's used by salesmen and people making demographic studies, and it is expensive, but for my purposes it is worth whatever it costs. *Cole's* is a telephone directory that lists every telephone number you would find in a regular telephone book, except *Cole's* lists them by street address as well as numerically. It's an expensive book, but you can buy year-old editions. For up-to-date stuff, however, all you can do is rent it for a year. The Manhattan *Cole's Directory* costs about $200. The Brooklyn and Queens books may run about $150, the Westchester book about $125, and so on. This is a book that returns its cost with one matrimonial.

"In matrimonial cases one of the first things that an injured party does—and it doesn't matter if it's the hus-

band or the wife—is that they begin going through the
monthly telephone bill looking for unusual numbers that
may have been called. After they've been through the
family telephone book and there are several numbers
that cannot be accounted for, those numbers are among
the first things they turn over to you as their private eye.
They certainly do not want to call those numbers and see
who they belong to, because of the suspicion it might
arouse. It becomes a job for the private eye. Actually all
I do is look up the numbers in the *Cole's Directory* and tell
them to whom the telephone is listed, and the address of
the person as well as every other telephone number
listed in that building. I can get up to $50 for every
telephone number I check. The same thing, of course, is
possible with the local telephone calls. You can request
a list of the local telephone calls made from your number
and the telephone company is obliged to give you sheets
that list, line by line, all of the calls made during a billing
period. I then do the same thing with the local calls. *Cole's*
keeps its library of directories on P Street in Lincoln,
Nebraska, and you can either write them or telephone
them for out-of-state numbers or address checks. For
each directory you rent you get two free requests a day.
If all you rent is a Bronx directory, you can call a New
York number with two requests a day regarding information anywhere in the city, including Westchester, Nassau,
and Suffolk. If I'm in court I can dial and get any information I need and make unlimited requests for information
from the directories I rent, which are unavailable to me
at the moment.

"The point is that there are an infinite number of
legitimate sources of information that are available to
just about anyone in this country. For two bucks I can
find out just about anything I want to know, not only
every lien ever imposed upon you and approved by a
court, but even how much you pay in property taxes. The
county clerk has your address listed by lot, on an asses-
sor's map. I can get the name of the owner of that lot,
the name of the person who holds the mortgage on that
lot, who held the previous mortgage, and how much is
being paid in taxes."

Blye takes out a five-page report he has just compiled
for a client. It was an investigation into the assets of a
very attractive thirty-five-year-old model who was being
kept by a wealthy seventy-year-old stockbroker. A few
years ago the broker had been listed as one of the ten
wealthiest men in New York. The broker's wife, a fifty-
year-old, fairly attractive Austrian woman to whom he
had been married for about twenty years, knew about the
affair her husband had been having with the model.
Since she herself was involved with a ski instructor at the
time and her husband denied her nothing, she was con-
tent enough with the arrangement. What the broker's
wife worried about, however, was the possibility that her
husband's infatuation with the young woman could
mushroom into the kind of emotional dependency that
might jeopardize her marriage and her income. The broker's wife, therefore, asked her attorney to hire a private
detective to find out just who her husband's mistress was,
how much he was giving her, and what, precisely, was the

nature of their relationship. The wife wanted most of all to be protected financially and to have evidence to use against her husband if and when he might initiate a divorce action.

"The woman didn't really care that her husband was having an affair with the model," Blye explains. "She just wanted to know how much the model was going to take the old man for when he died. She said that she didn't mind as long as the girl didn't get more than about a million bucks. Since the old man was estimated to have about $75 million, that obviously left enough for her and her ski instructor.

"What she wanted was for me to check the model's finances," Blye continues, "but she didn't want anyone tipped that she was doing any checking up on her own. In other words, if a lawyer wanted an income evaluation or credit check on someone he might go to firms such as Proudfoot or Bishop's and for about $350 or $500 get an exhaustive analysis. The only problem with these outfits is that they insist upon interviewing the person being investigated and the law reads that if the subject of their inquiries wants a copy of the report themselves, it must be made available.

"A private detective will try to amass the same amount of information, for about the same amount of money, maybe a little more, but we will do it in such a way that the subjects will never know they're being checked up on. We use the regular sources of information. Private detectives have contacts within credit bureaus or banks or credit card firms who will Xerox our subject's applica-

tion for $25 a sheet. There are lots of sources, lots of
techniques, and they all change constantly depending
upon who you're talking to. The personality of the clerk,
bank official, credit manager, postal employee, whoever
you happen to need, is critical. You have got to somehow
get these people interested in your case. Even if you pass
along money you still have to make up some kind of a
story. You're looking for somebody because they've
been left some money, their mother is dying, any kind of
a story that might give the bureaucrat you've slipped a
few bucks to some incentive."

The report about the ex-model, with Blye's com-
ments, follows:

BELLMORE, HOLLY
New York, N.Y., 735 East 9th Street.

Investigation in this matter was conducted in an
effort to determine assets of the subject, with the
following results:

The subject currently occupies apartment #5, on
the ground floor of an 11-story apartment building
at 735 East 9th Street, New York. This is a five-room
apartment shared by the subject and her son, who
is reported to be about 11 or 12 years old. The
apartment is owned by Mrs. Bellmore. She has
owned the apartment for approximately three years
and management officials, while refusing to be specific regards the purchase price, have stated it is
valued in excess of $50,000.

"Most of that information," Blye explains, "came from the building's manager. I just called the guy up and said I was making a credit inquiry. I said that a Mrs. Holly Bellmore had applied for credit and had given 735 East 9th Street as her address and said it was a cooperative apartment. In other words, as you talk to the guy you set him up. You sound as official as hell and slightly bored. If you already know so much, most of these people feel, there's nothing wrong with giving you a little more. I asked, for instance, how long had she been living in the apartment. I asked where she had been previously living. He had her original application for the apartment and he gave me her previous address. What harm? he might think, but her previous address would give me a new area to poke around in. I asked how many occupants in her apartment. How many rooms. I got the names of references, the rent or maintenance she paid, and the names of her banks. It always amazes me how easy it is. Once you get past the initial hesitancy and appear to have a totally legitimate need for the information, people almost always help. The bait that you dangle out there, of course, is the fact that maybe the person you're checking up on is a deadbeat, or is about to go bust. Even the most straitlaced business people want to know if someone they extend credit to is having trouble. I suspect that one of the reasons lots of these people keep talking is that they're trying to figure out from what I'm asking whether they have anything to worry about."

Prior to occupying the apartment, the subject is reported to have lived briefly at the nearby Fifth Avenue Hotel and before that, resided with her husband, Joseph V. Bellmore, in a rented apartment at 2112 East 86th Street, N.Y.C., where they leased apartment 5B from approximately 1970.

"The old broker had really taken care of Holly well," Blye continues. "He had apparently set her up with a $50,000-a-year income, bought her the apartment, and gave her occasional presents, but his wife wanted to know whether he was funneling any big money in her direction. I was getting $125 a day for an eight-hour stint and I usually worked with one of my guys if we were going to put in a night watching the old guy and his girl friend. He'd pick her up in the limo and then they'd go somewhere good and expensive to eat. Lutèce. Brussels. Four Seasons. The Coach House. Those kinds of places. I'd wait outside and follow them when they left. It never failed. They would go back to her apartment on Ninth Street about 11:30 and the old guy would leave by midnight."

Earlier, she is reported to have lived in Charon, Conn., where informants advise us she was born.

"Charon, Connecticut, is a really small town. I remember I got some background on Holly by going up there and talking to some of the local merchants. I said I was a reporter and that I was doing an article on why people were leaving New York. I talked to people on the street where she had lived and picked up just about all I needed. There was also a Charon Library where I could have found local newspapers and that kind of stuff. High school year books. Hometown girl makes good as a big city model. That kind of thing."

At this writing we learn of no employment for the subject, though in the past she had dabbled in the modeling business. A few years ago she was being booked through the Chic Fashion Agency, of 110 West 67th Street, New York. She was earning $40.00 an hour when she worked. Earlier, she had also worked sporadically through the Frances Brill Agency of 15 Madison Avenue, New York. During her modeling career, she worked under the name of Holly Ann Penny.

"I found out she was a model from the wife's lawyer. It wouldn't have been hard. Everyone in the building where she lived knew she had been a model. The lawyer also had a picture of her that had appeared in a maga-zine. I called the magazine and got the name of the model agency that handled that specific account. I said that I was putting out a catalogue and wanted some of the same models as had appeared in the magazine arti-cle. All I wanted to know was the cost. It was the model agency that said Holly Bellmore was Holly Ann Penny and that her fee, along with the other models handled by the agency, was $40 an hour."

In local credit circles, the subject is favorably regarded as a credit risk and has maintained accounts
at the following: W & J Sloane, Gimbels, Bloomingdale's, Henri Bendel, Bergdorf Goodman, Saks
Fifth Avenue, B. Altman, Lord and Taylor, Bonwit
Teller, and Sears Roebuck. It is interesting to note
that in the latter part of 1974 ["about the time that
she moved into the apartment and was set up by the
old man"], she apparently opened several of these
accounts in a very short time. Credit Bureau files
reveal there were inquiries on her during that period, as follows: 10-16-74, Henri Bendel inquired.
On same date, Bergdorf Goodman inquired. Eight
days later it was Saks Fifth Avenue. Then on 12-
11-74, B. Altman inquired; 12-13-74, Lord and Taylor. Her bills are usually paid on a 30-60 day basis.
It was also noted that she is known to some of the
stores under the name of Sarah Bellmore. Her telephone listing is maintained as H. Bellmore.

"That was easier to find out than you might think,"
Blye says. "I just called a friend of mine who specializes
in credit reporting. He works for hotels and stores and
anyone who has to extend credit to strangers. There are
lots of guys like my friend. Just about every private investigator knows a couple of people who work in credit
reporting agencies. You give them between $25 and $50
per credit check and it saves a lot of work.
    "If for some reason I had to do the credit check on my
own," Blye continues, "I would check with one of the

stores in which I knew she had a credit card or with a local merchant or bank. I'd just call them, identify myself, and say that Holly Bellmore of 735 East 9th Street has applied for credit and that she has listed your store or bank as a reference. I act a little rushed. I imply that we are willing to extend the credit, but that she is going to claim whatever it is she is buying within the hour. If she has good credit, people will usually be helpful. If not, merchants and even bankers are very broad in hinting that the person you're calling about may be a dud.

"There is also the good old UCC-1 form that puts on file at the city registry office every outstanding loan made by anyone in the city. If I see that she has an outstanding loan with Chase, I note the branch number. If I see she has an outstanding loan with smaller finance companies then I know I'll get everything I need. Finance office managers work pretty much on their own, and because of the risk in the kind of loans they extend, they insist upon a tremendous amount of information. Some privates will even call the local finance manager, pretending to be from one of the banks where she has a loan, and ask for the credit information. If the manager gives them any trouble they remind him that his district boss is always calling the bank for information and that it's too tough a job if guys in the same business don't help each other out in a pinch. Most privates use whatever line they think will work. They use them as the situations arise and as the character of the person they're talking to reveals itself."

A check of other available records, including voter registrations, reveals she has voted under the name of Holly Ann Bellmore. She is a registered member of the Liberal party and her permanent voting registration number is #3037632. Voting records reflect her date of birth as Dec. 27, 1933, and when she voted in 1964 she indicated she had been living in the State of New York for only three years. Her husband, at that time, Joseph Bellmore, from whom she is since reported to have been divorced, also voted and his occupation was listed as "Bible salesman." Husband was also registered as a Liberal and his registration number is #2079823. Joseph Bellmore's current whereabouts are not known but we understand he had encountered financial difficulties prior to the divorce and there were various federal tax liens outstanding against him. This is interesting in the light of the fact that the subject gives building employees at the apartment house where she resides the impression she is able to live so comfortably and without working because she received such a generous settlement from her ex-husband. She also contends she receives substantial alimony payments. A summary of the federal tax liens against her ex-husband are as follows:

9-25-72	$2,063.03	Fed Tax Lein Register #435a
11-26-72	$2,369.15	Fed Tax Lien Register #4731
2-11-73	$1,893.60	Fed Tax Lien Register #832

All of the above were served at 1 1 2 East 86th Street, New York.

"All of that stuff was public record," Blye continues, "even Holly and her husband's voting registration. I got that by going down to the Board of Elections and getting one of the clerks to get off their ass and help. Everyone who is registered to vote is registered by their election district. If you know someone's address you can ask to see their registration in that election district. It is public knowledge. No great big secret. The only secret is in somehow getting the Board of Elections clerk to help you. If not, if you don't get them interested in what you're doing, they wander off and say they can't find the book. They say you should come back tomorrow when the regular guy is on. They say their coffee break is coming up and somebody else will help you. It's a regular zoo with everyone trying to duck any kind of work at all.

"If you get people interested, though, if you get them to think that what they're doing is good and that it's really helping someone in trouble and that they would want someone to give a little extra if they needed the help, it's surprising how the same bored bureaucrats can respond. I usually use the one about how I'm trying to locate somebody who has just come into some money. Or, I'll use the one about locating someone because their mother is dying and can't reach them. Anything, just as long as the person with whom you're working cares about helping you find what you're looking for.

"Tax liens are, of course, public information and

they're available in any county courthouse," Blye goes on. "But on the nonpublic information, you've got to know the language. If I call a bank, for instance, I don't ask for the credit department, because they usually give you short shrift. I'll usually ask for the manager and get one of his assistants. I'll give them the story about checking on a prospective customer's credit and that she gave the bank as a recommendation. Usually they'll tell you when she established her account and if it is a satisfactory account. I might then ask if there are any accommodations—that's bank talk for loans—and in a few seconds we're usually chatting about the account. Sometimes I'll say that I'm calling from a super-private club and that the subject has made an application, citing the bank as a reference. Once they sense that you know something about the person you're asking about, just about everyone loosens up a little.

"The toughest place to get information, however, is not from banks and credit companies," Blye says, "but from hospitals. They are so paranoid over lawsuits and malpractice and every horror you can imagine that all they'll ever give you is the fact that a person is a patient and their condition. The way some shady characters get around that is to call up and say they're doctors. Hospitals are programmed to jump whenever they hear the word 'doctor.' It's like Pavlov's drooling dog."

A check of the litigation dockets for the subject reveals no suits or judgments against her.

"That came out of the same place that the liens against her husband turned up."

A check of several of the local banks revealed the subject maintains an account with the Bank of New York office at 530 Fifth Avenue, New York. The account is under the name of Holly Bellmore ["I found that out from her department store credit references"] and she has had the account since August of 1974. The account is described as being a highly satisfactory regular checking account, with an average balance in the medium five figures.

"In bank talk that means she had about $13,000 in a regular checking account drawing no interest," Blye says. "No wonder they called it 'highly satisfactory.' It also means that she gives them no trouble. No overdrafts. No telephone calls late in the afternoon about expected overdrafts. I got that information by telling the bank they had been used as a reference."

We have also made inquiry at several of the leading brokerage houses to determine if the subject has such accounts. These inquiries, however, have been negative. We were advised by brokerage firms that the subject had no accounts under her own name or any of the other variations on her name we had encountered during the investigation.

"That was what the broker's wife really wanted to know about," Blye says. "Since her husband was in the brokerage business she was afraid he might have been funneling some money, lots of money, into his girl friend's pocketbook through the market. For a man like him it would have been easy. I'd call the brokerages claiming to be a credit rating service and say I wanted to verify the Holly Bellmore account. When they said they didn't have one for Holly Bellmore, I'd say Sarah and keep it up until I was sure there wasn't an account in her name or his. In the end, it is always a matter of knowing how to deal with personalities on the phone. You've got to be constantly tuned to other people's wavelengths, picking up whatever hints you can find. Are they the type to break rules? Will they do it on this occasion? Can they be bullied? Can they be conned? It's manipulative of people as hell, but providing every one of your competitors knows where the information can be found, the game will be won by whoever has the greatest con."

8 It was a cold January morning and the drive out to eastern Long Island in search of a barmaid and Tiny Berels's carnival-working, beer-drinking pals meant an hour of squinting into a rising sun. If Blye could prove that Tiny had indeed been in New York on June 24, Tiny would probably be acquitted, but it would require unimpeachable testimony and irrefutable evidence. The case against Tiny was tough. Wanda Moore swore that Tiny was the fat man who kidnapped her at knifepoint from the shopping center parking lot in Spartanburg. After escaping from her captors, Edna had given the police a detailed description of the men who had held her for more than eight hours. But, according

to Bob Faucette's letter to Irwin Blye and according to
the information Blye had just picked up at his office,
there were some discrepancies between her description
of the man who kidnapped her and Tiny Berels.

FEDERAL BUREAU OF INVESTIGATION
Date of transcription: June 27, 1975
Spec. Agent Walter L. Lake
  Moore described the man who forced her into the
car as follows:
  White male, possibly late twenties or early thirties, six feet to six feet three inches, 300 or more
pounds, sandy brown hair, medium length, curly,
greasy; full, curly beard and mustache covering
cheeks.
  She stated she noticed he was grossly fat with
rolls of fat on arms, stomach, and neck; round un-
lined moon face, thick lips, wheezing voice, heavy
sweating, ruddy red complexion; spoke in "backwoods" southern dialect, ungrammatically; black
hair on arms, no jewelry. He was dressed in blue
short-sleeved shirt, stained with sweat rings, possibly jeans pants.

"While Tiny is over six feet tall and weighs in excess
of 300 pounds," Faucette's letter to Blye began, "he has
black hair, wavy, not curly. His arms are firm and do not
have rolls of fat. His neck is also firm. He has an oblong
rather than moon face. He has thin lips, not thick, and
he does not wheeze when he talks. He has a fair, rather
ruddy complexion and he does not speak in a deep 'back-

woods' southern dialect. He has very noticeable tattoos on both arms and a small dot tattooed approximately one inch below his right eye.

"According to the enclosed FBI interview with Edna," Faucette's letter continued, "she made no mention of her kidnapper having any tattoos. Considering the complete nature of her description it is unlikely that she wouldn't have mentioned such a characteristic if the kidnapper had them.

"The indictment alleges that Berels kidnapped Edna Kay Moore on June 24, in Spartanburg, South Carolina, and transported her to Charlotte, North Carolina. The trip took approximately eight (8) hours.

"During June that year, Berels claims that he was working for Harry Fried who operates Carnival Amusements, Inc. Berels was running several concessions for Carnival Amusements, Inc. At the time of the offense the carnival was playing in Lake Ronkonkoma, New York. The carnival played at Lake Ronkonkoma for approximately 18 days. Prior to coming to Lake Ronkonkoma, the carnival was located in Islip, Long Island. Berels believes that the carnival was in Lake Ronkonkoma on June 24.

"While there," the Faucette letter continued, "Berels frequently went to the Grove Bar or Grove Tavern. The Grove Tavern, he says, is run by a female named Murray. There is a waitress at the Grove Bar whose first name is Patty and she should know Berels. He apparently became a good friend of hers while he was at Lake Ronkonkoma. Patty is heavy, short, and has brown-black hair.

They called Berels 'Tiny' at the Grove Bar.

"About a block from the Grove Bar there is a shopping center with three to six stores. It should be a small shopping center. Berels told me that he ate at a café in the shopping center frequently and that the man that ran the café was short and wore glasses and should remember him.

"While Berels was in Lake Ronkonkoma he stayed with an individual who has a first name of Charlie. Charlie is an old man with no teeth and is probably receiving a disability check. He had a wood frame house which was approximately two and one half miles from the bar. Charlie apparently drinks a great deal.

"After Berels was fired by the carnival," the letter continued, "he stayed around until he was able to get enough money to buy a train ticket to Philadelphia, Pennsylvania. You will note that the ticket was dated July 1, 1975. Berels also tells me that during this time he did not have a beard or mustache as Edna Moore described and he said he can also verify that he had his teeth pulled in January of that year and did not get his new ones until August—another very obvious characteristic that the observant Edna Moore failed to note in her description of her abductor.

"We need to obtain signed statements from the witnesses that can verify Berels was in New York during the time the alleged kidnapping took place. Under federal rules I can subpoena these witnesses and require them to come to Columbia, South Carolina. The government will have to pay their expenses since Berels is an indigent defendant. It is my understanding that the FBI has done some investigating and has, in fact, talked with Harry Fried. I understand that they were a little vague because they were paying Berels in cash and not keeping a record."

It was a better and far more complete letter than Irwin Blye usually receives from lawyers getting paid about $750 by the government to defend indigent clients. Actually, Bob Faucette should get paid $30 an hour for defending Tiny, but most federal district judges put an arbitrary limit on the amount of money court-appointed lawyers can receive. Private detectives in such cases receive $15 an hour with a $250 cut-off. The lawyer forwards to the private investigator a CJA-21 voucher he receives from the local federal district court. The private detective then fills in his name, Social Security number, and the hours he worked on the specific case. He mails the voucher to the deputy clerk of the federal district court, and within a month or two, if the judge or court officials feel his request for compensation is proper, he receives a check from the government in payment of his fee. In cases involving state courts such as New York's, rather than CJA-21 vouchers, the private detective is paid as an 18-B employee of the court. The 18-B designation alludes to the section of the state law that entitles indigent defendants appearing in state courts to the services of attorneys and, when necessary, private detectives.

Blye had spent about an hour in his office poring over Bob Faucette's letter, checking out some of the suggested avenues of inquiry. As usual, nothing was quite what the Faucette letter made it seem. For instance, the letter clearly said that Tiny frequented the Grove Bar or Grove Tavern on Lake Ronkonkoma Avenue and that there was a female barmaid or waitress named Patty and a woman owner.

"Never go anywhere without checking the address," Blye said, while dialing the information operator for Long Island. He smiled when the operator said there was no Grove Tavern or Bar in Lake Ronkonkoma.

Next, Blye called the Suffolk County police, learning that Lake Ronkonkoma is in the fourth precinct, which he called.

No, they had never heard of a Grove Bar or Tavern, but perhaps he should call the sixth precinct, as well. They cover the same area and they might know.

The sixth precinct had never heard of the Grove Tavern or Grove Bar, either. Tiny's alibi was getting weaker and Blye had not even left his office.

Blye then asked the police for the names of various bars they knew that were in Lake Ronkonkoma and the patrolman on the switchboard obliged. None of them, he assured Blye, sounded even remotely like the place he was looking for and none of them were run by women.

Blye thanked the patrolman and hung up. Then he called the Lake Ronkonkoma information operator again and got the telephone numbers for the bars and grills the police had given him. There was no answer to his first two calls, but on the third call a cleaning man answered. He said the Grove Bar or Tavern could be the Orange

Grove Bar, but it had recently changed its name. Yes, the man told Blye, it was owned by a woman. He knew her name. Helen Mann. He had worked for her. The bar that Helen owned was now known as the Good Time Bar and Grill.

The telephone information operator gave Blye the number and the address. He called.

"Hello?"

"Is this the Good Time Bar?" Blye asked.

"Yes."

"Is Mrs. Helen Mann there?"

"I'm Helen."

"Mrs. Mann, my name is Irwin Blye and I represent a man who says he was a customer of your bar. Leo Timothy Berels."

"Who? I don't—"

"He's also known as Tiny and—"

"Oh, Tiny," Mrs. Mann said. "Sure, I know Tiny."

"Well, Mrs. Mann, Tiny has gotten himself in a little trouble in South Carolina and you might be able to help him."

"What can I do?"

"Tiny says that he was in New York, working with the carnival at Lake Ronkonkoma last June 24. If we can prove that, it will clear him of some charges against him in South Carolina."

"I can't swear by the exact dates right now, but he was here that summer and I think he had to be here in June."

"Did he know a barmaid at your place named Patty?"

"Patty, sure. She'll be able to help you. She and Tiny

were good friends. What kind of trouble is Tiny in?"

"He's been arrested for kidnapping."

"Tiny? Impossible. He's just a big kid. He was just a big softie. He was as gentle as he was big."

After getting Patty's home address from Helen, Blye made an appointment to meet her at the Good Time Bar around noon. She would be willing to help him in any way she could. Tiny, she insisted, might not have been too bright, but he was not a violent man and was not the kind of person who would ever harm anyone.

Blye next called Harry Fried, the co-owner of Carnival Amusements, Inc., and Tiny Berels's employer in New York. Fried was wary.

"Who do you represent?" he asked. "Who do you work for?"

Blye said he was working for attorneys representing a former employee, Tiny Berels, who had been charged with kidnapping in South Carolina on June 24, a day the defendant claims he was working in New York.

"I already spoke to the FBI," Fried said. "I couldn't verify the last day he worked for me. The best information I had was that his last day was either June 23, 24, or 25."

"Did you see him after his last day?" Blye asked.

"After his last day I didn't see him for a couple of days," Fried said. "But then I wasn't looking for him either. We let him go, you know. There was a little argument. He was working one of our joints, that's one of the booths at the concession, and he was taking more nickels, dimes, and quarters than he should have."

"Tiny says through his attorney that he was in New York at the time," Blye said. "Is there any way we can verify that fact through your records?"

"I can't verify it. I even told the FBI that Tiny's last day was either the 23, 24, or 25," Fried said. "It was any of those three days. I couldn't narrow it down any better than that."

Fried was adamant. Eventually, Blye thanked him and hung up.

Blye often runs into trouble confirming specific dates of employment for indigent clients.

"Even when they do work," Blye explains, "the people who hire them usually pay them 'off the books,' which means they are paid by cash on a daily or weekly basis with no records being kept. This way the employer does not have to comply with workmen's compensation laws, he doesn't have to deal with withholding taxes and insurance. The worker is happy because he's getting paid in cash and doesn't have to report it as income and possibly jeopardize some welfare or unemployment benefits he might be getting at the same time. One of the biggest problems in this business is convincing people that we are not looking to mess up their little larcenies. I've talked with people who would just as soon see some innocent man go to the electric chair as lose their rent subsidy or welfare check or admit they paid their employees off the books."

9

Driving toward Lake Ronkonkoma, Blye considered Tiny's chances. Harry Fried, the carnival owner, was a washout. Helen, the owner of the Good Time Bar, sounded as though she might be helpful, but bar owners, drinking companions, and carnival workers were not the kinds of unimpeachable witnesses one needed to beat down the testimony of Tiny's nineteen-year-old accuser. Blye was hoping, however, that Tiny's pals and drinking buddies would lead him to other sources, such as merchants and landlords who might have sold Tiny something on June 24, 1975. He was looking for some kind of legal and binding business transaction that would hold up in court.

And yet, there were things about the prosecution's case against Tiny that Blye did not like. The FBI description, for instance, which was supplied by Edna Moore, was as curious for what it lacked as for what it contained. While she described in detail the rolls of fat on the man's arms, she forgot to mention any tattoos. She had also failed to note that he was toothless. A dentist's letter that Faucette had sent Blye said Tiny had no teeth in his head from January until August of that year. Why hadn't Edna mentioned that? Could she be mistaken?

While Blye had at first felt it was hard to be uncertain about a three-hundred-pound kidnapper after you've been in the rear seat of a car for approximately eight hours, he began to have second thoughts when he read the police report about how Tiny Berels had been arrested. Tiny, it turned out, wasn't arrested shortly after the kidnapping incident took place, but on November 9, almost six months after Edna Moore's abduction.

Descriptions, like potato salad at a picnic, go bad with time. Tiny had apparently been arrested by the Dallas, North Carolina, Police Department as the result of an FBI flyer which was circulated with a composite sketch of Edna's kidnapper and a description. Tiny had been living in a trailer park on the outskirts of Dallas, about thirty miles from Charlotte, when he was arrested by the Dallas police. Berels, they said, fit the description of the kidnapper to the pound. The next day, when Tiny was brought before the Charlotte police, Edna Moore, without hesitancy, identified him as the man who kidnapped her on June 24. Within two days Tiny was indicted by a

federal grand jury for kidnapping and was arraigned before Judge Robert Chapel, a crusty member of one of
Spartanburg's first families. Tiny, protesting his innocence, was held on $10,000 bail and given the services
of Charlotte attorney Robert Faucette.

Edna Moore could have been wrong. The carnival
people might not be able to prove that Tiny was employed on June 24, but they certainly substantiated his
claim that he was in New York during that period. Also,
according to Faucette's letter, Tiny did not want to cop
a plea and draw a lighter sentence by implicating the two
men who were supposed to have been in the car with
him. There were no two men, he insisted. There was no
kidnapping.

In the summer Lake Ronkonkoma is a workingman's
resort, the Bar Harbor of the Archie Bunker set, but in
the winter it is a bitterly cold, grim place. Lake Ronkonkoma Avenue, where Blye expected to find the Good
Time Bar, is plastered with beware-of-dog and house-to-
let signs and yellow and red billboards advertising pre-
cast cesspools for $250. A cold wind blows across the
nearly frozen five-square-mile lake, shaking the screen
doors and windows on the town's dilapidated frame
houses, tool sheds, and homemade garages. Backyards
and driveways are cluttered with the peeling hulls of
battered boats forlornly awaiting the summer months.
The automobiles Blye passed on the avenue were old
and the men inside them were huddled against the cold
in thick mackinaws and caps. Automobile heaters didn't
work in Lake Ronkonkoma.

There was a Hardee Hamburger stand and a Grant Plaza shopping center, but bankruptcy signs were pasted in most of the center's store windows. What Lake Ronkonkoma had, however, was bars. There was Connor's Pub and the Fireman's Pub. There was the Pleasure Lounge and the Pizza Lounge. It was shortly before noon on a sunbright, cold January Monday and each of the town's bars seemed to have at least three or four beat-up cars parked on the gravel between the road and the front door.

The Good Time Bar had a hand-lettered sign in the window that read: "Hot and Cold Lunches." It was a frame shack with bent metal Coke signs nailed to its walls and neon beer signs hanging in its tiny windows. On the gravel in front of the Good Time Bar were four beat-up wrecks and a panel truck from a local plumbing supply firm. The sun was high and bounced off the sheet of ice that covered the gray lake behind the bar. Cottages, shacks, and rickety piers jutted into the lake from the shore. Behind the bar the wooden platform from which its summertime guests could drink their beer while looking out over the water was deserted except for a frozen mop and pail.

Helen Mann was standing at the end of the long dark bar next to the cash register. The place smelled of last night's spilled beer. None of the men at the bar had more than a dollar and change in front of them. Their conversation ceased as Blye walked into the room. They were workingmen, hard thick fingers with nails chipped and blackened from years of heavy construction and industrial work. They sipped their beers from tall fluted glasses with surprising delicacy to avoid spillage.

Helen Mann was gray-haired, fifty-six years old, and from the way she looked at her clientele, Blye got the feeling she was sorry she and her husband ever bought the Good Time. She had the strong look of a no-nonsense businesswoman and the manner in which she dispatched a beer delivery man while talking with Blye made it obvious. She took the detective to a small table in the back of the bar where, sipping coffee from a paper container, she told him about Tiny.

"You wouldn't forget him," she said. "He was over six feet tall and weighed more than three hundred pounds. He also had an earring, a small gold earring through— I think it was his right ear.

"We had taken over the bar just before the summer when the carnival came. I remember that period, believe me, because I had just broken my wrist and had my whole left arm in a cast. That's when I had to hire some help and I hired Patricia Boyle. I looked up the date. It was June 16. Patricia, that's your Patty, stayed with me until August 18, and it was Patricia, or Patty, who was friendly with Tiny during that period."

As Helen talked Blye listened intently and occasionally took notes. A date, a name and nickname, curious items to be checked further. No one, for instance, had ever mentioned that Tiny wore an earring. Edna Moore hadn't mentioned it and neither had Tiny's lawyer.

"I knew the guy, he used to come in every night," Helen said. "Let me tell you, he was a baby. A pussycat.

He was as soft as he was big. He was like a child. I've been around bars, I know people, and Tiny was just a big kid. First, I really don't think he had all the brains he needed. I mean, I think he may have been a little retarded. Not too much, but a little. I say that because people could take advantage of him, kid him, joke around at his expense, and he never really minded.

"All he wanted was to be liked and for the people around him to have a good time. And I saw him sober and I saw him falling down drunk and he was always the same. Kidnapping girls? It's hard to believe. He wasn't the type. Even when drunk you'd never see him get out of line. He never leered or made wisecracks or was dirty sexy, if you know what I mean. He used to joke with Patty about them being fat, but she did most of the joking, and since she enjoyed the kidding around, so did Tiny. Things come out when a guy gets drunk and you see things about people that you don't usually see. I used to watch all the time. It's my business. A guy Tiny's size you especially watch, because God forbid he becomes trouble, you need an army of cops to put him away, and in all those months and all my looking he never once was out of line in the least. That's why kidnapping just doesn't make sense. I would have to say it wasn't in him."

"Helen, I'm going to show you a copy of Tiny's North Carolina driver's license," Blye said, smiling encouragingly at the bar owner. "Is that Tiny?"

Helen took the copy of Tiny's license and his photograph that Bob Faucette had routinely sent along for identification purposes.

"Sure," she said, "that's Tiny."

"How do you think we can prove Tiny was here during June and specifically on June twenty-four?" Blye asked. "He's really depending upon you people. It's a matter of proving he was here. What makes you think he was here?"

"I know Tiny was hanging around the bar before the carnival opened. It opened in the beginning of June. I don't remember the exact date."

Blye knew. He had gotten the date, June 7, from Harry Fried, the carnival owner, during their conversation.

"And I also know he was still here when the carnival closed," Helen continued. "He was here at least until August and I can't remember not seeing him for more than a day or two. He'd come to the bar every day after work. He'd talk with Patty and they'd joke about the fact that they were both so fat that they couldn't do anything."

"Helen," Blye began solemnly, "what you've told me could very well help Tiny. Would you mind signing a statement to what you've just told me? And, if the lawyers need you to testify on Tiny's behalf, would you be able to fly down to the trial at the court's expense?"

"Yes," Helen said, "I would."

Blye then took out a three-ply pad of ruled writing paper with carbons. The words "Irwin Blye Investigations 299 Broadway, N.Y., N.Y." were printed across the top of every sheet. He began to write in ball-point pen, reading to Helen every word he was writing in her name.

On this the 6th day of January 1975 I Helen Mann, married, say that I am fifty-six (56) years of age and residing . . .

As Blye read one sentence after another to Helen she would nod her assent.

. . . During the summer of 1975 a carnival came into this town. A man who was white, wore one earring, was very heavy, over six feet tall, weighed in excess of three hundred pounds, came into the Good Time Bar almost every day. The carnival was located just west of us on the opposite side of the Bavarian Inn. He was known to us as Tiny. I had broken my left wrist and it was in a cast. I hired a barmaid, Patricia Boyle, known as Patty, everyone called her Patty. . . .

At that point Blye came to the bottom of his first page of ruled paper. He asked Helen to read it again and asked her to sign the first page. She did. The statement-taking continued:

I hired her on June 16, 1975, she worked until August 18, 1975. She was friendly with Tiny. I first recall seeing Tiny when they first set up the carnival. He was here at least until August. I don't know if the carnival was still in town at that time. I am being shown a picture of Tiny on an operator's license number 4937843. The name on the license is Leo Timothy Berels of Dallas, N.C.

"Thank you, Helen," Blye said, after rereading the entire statement to her. He then began numbering every one of the statement's ruled lines.

"Now, Helen, would you mind writing yourself that you have read the above two pages and thirty-seven lines and understand each and every line and know them to be true?"

"Of course," said Helen.

Despite the fact that fictional private investigators are never depicted going through the drudgery of taking statements from potential witnesses, the taking of statements is one of the most important parts of the private eye's job. The techniques employed to get reluctant people to talk vary with detectives.

"I don't have any set routine in getting statements," Blye says. "A lot of the stuff in the business is instinct and intuition. You can get a feeling about certain people and how they want you to act. In this job you accommodate.

"You can't make people feel inferior. You can't make them feel subservient. Whenever people offer me anything like a cup of coffee or anything, I always accept. I've had to drink coffee out of cracked cups with roach wings floating around inside, but I've noticed that poor people, especially poor people, are very sensitive about whether or not a guy with a briefcase and a necktie will eat at their table. It's often the ice-breaker. Once you've drunk from their dirty cups they have a tendency of immediately warming up to you. Poor people, once they feel you're not trying to screw them or look down upon them, are always the most helpful and kindest.

"The other important thing about statements and getting witnesses to cooperate," Blye continues, "is to make sure they know that you are trying to help somebody. I am trying to help Tiny. Tiny is in trouble. Maybe he's being falsely accused. I'm trying to help him. I'm a good samaritan and I need their help too. Helping people is the operative word. People understand that. The longshoreman understands that. The bartender understands that. They know what it is like to be harassed and caught up in powerful forces.

"There's a little bit of con involved, but mostly it's a matter of getting the people you're talking to to get involved in seeing that an injustice is not done. You see, everybody's a hero in their own heads, and if you can slice in on them at their hero level, even the nastiest types are usually helpful.

"Some privates make the mistake of telling potential witnesses that their clients are innocent," Blye says, "but most people are too smart for that. They don't know any better than I do whether Tiny or anyone else is guilty or not. People become suspicious when the hard sell is used.

"I don't hard sell. I admit that I don't know if Tiny did it or not. There's a chance he did, but then there's a chance that he didn't and all that I'm asking for is a little help just in case he didn't. I ask people to give my clients the same chance they would want."

Blye thanked Helen again and said he wanted a picture of her for the lawyer. She blushed a little and smiled.

Blye went to the trunk of his car where he took out a ten-year-old Polaroid camera and photographed Helen standing in front of the entrance to the Good Time Bar.

"You've been a real help, Helen, thanks again," Blye said. "I just hope that Patty can be as helpful."

"Yeah, I hope so too," Helen said. "Nobody wants to see the wrong guy go away for something."

"That's all we want to do, Helen. Make sure the wrong guy doesn't go to jail."

"Oh!" Helen suddenly said, as though remembering a point she intended making earlier. "You know the picture you showed me of Tiny on his driver's license?"

"Yes," Blye said.

"Well, it was Tiny all right, except when he was here that whole summer he was wearing a bushy beard."

Driving toward Patty's, Blye kept thinking about Helen describing Tiny with a beard. That fit Edna Moore's description of the man who abducted her. Also, while Helen confirmed that Tiny was drinking in Lake Ronkonkoma just about every night during the period in question, she could give no proof that he was in her place on June 24. She even had to admit that there were occasionally one-to-two-day periods when she didn't see him at all. The fact that she was a responsible business person, however, made her a good potential witness and the fact that she could place Tiny, except for brief periods, in Lake Ronkonkoma during the time of the abduction could help. But Patty, Blye thought, would have to be better.

10

Irwin Blye grew up on Broadway. Times Square was his Sesame Street. He was raised behind the Blye Shop, a men's haberdashery on the southwest corner of Broadway and 51st Street. The store was owned by his uncles Paul and Arnold, but it was run by his father, Lawrence. Young Blye spent his after-school hours and his Saturdays with his father at the store. It was a unique environment in which to raise a youngster but it bestowed upon young Blye a street sense that has been an invaluable aid in his chosen profession. After having spent his eleventh to eighteenth years in Times Square, Irwin Blye is not only con-proof, he does not even have to prove it.

Blye spent his formative years, during the late forties and early fifties, roaming around in a Guys and Dolls New York. For instance, across from the Blye Shop, on the northwest corner, was the city's show biz, gambling, and cheesecake capital, Lindy's. On the northeast side of the intersection bookmaker Champ Segal had his steak joint where most of the city's serious gamblers, including Frank Costello, some cloak and suiters, and a few friendly judges, dined and wagered regularly. Detectives in $100 suits ($400 at today's prices) from the West 47th Street precinct would show up to see the big winners safely home. On the southeast corner of that Runyonesque intersection was the Ham 'n' Eggery, a twenty-four-hour-a-day hangout that catered to street hustlers, show girls, actors, reporters, hotel managers, district leaders, firemen, racketeers, cops, columnists, comedians, bookies, ex-pugs, jazz musicians, loan sharks, waiters, hit men, ticket scalpers, and Tammany judges. It was also a place where Irwin Blye had a charge account at the age of twelve. In a neighborhood bereft of children, young Irwin was a local favorite under the benign gaze of some of the scariest men in America.

When other youngsters his age were aspiring to Eagle Scouthood and memorizing twenty-seven life-saving knots, little Irwin was learning about shaving dice and basketball point spreads. Broadway merchants, from the papaya-juice-and-hot-dog man to Jack Dempsey seated in his restaurant window, kept an eye on Blye. Broadway characters such as Milton Berle and Henny Youngman, as well as noncomedians like Danny St. John and Frank

Costello, looked on Irwin as a mascot. Even Leo Lindy, that irascible restaurateur, enjoyed sending young Blye to Milton Berle's crowded center table with folded messages. The messages were, of course, insulting, vile, and unsigned. Berle, who never minded the ritual of a joke as long as he kept the spotlight, would carefully examine the note handed to him by the solemn-faced kid. Irwin had gone through the routine so many times that he knew his part clean. Berle would erupt into one of his manic parodies of madness in an effort to force a smile on the face of the straightman messenger. At eleven, Blye was playing second banana to Milton Berle. He would kid Mel Tormé by calling him Vic Damone. Jackie Robinson gave him passes to see the Dodgers play the Giants at the old Polo Grounds. Blye hated the Dodgers and refused to go to Brooklyn's Ebbets Field to watch them play, despite the fact that Robinson was a good customer at his father's store.

Tom Mackel, who later became the Queens County district attorney, was the cop on the beat in front of the Blye Shop. Kid Gavilan, the fighter, was a regular at the store as were singers Billy Daniels and Tony Martin. Blye remembers being slipped into the Copa through the basement kitchen and past the Chinese cooks to watch Billy Daniels. He also remembers his high school prom when the maître d' at Bill Miller's Riviera, suspiciously eyeing the no-tip high school kids, refused to honor their reservations. Blye went to a phone, called the Riviera stage entrance and asked for Tony Martin. Blye then told his father's customer about the problem he was having outside and Martin said not to worry. Blye returned to his friends, who were growing anxious as they watched one party of adults after another being led to tables.

"Within a few minutes the maître d' came out," Blye says, "and asked for Mr. Blye. We were walked right in. It was wonderful. It should happen to every kid on his prom night."

While still a youngster, Blye knew people from the Carousel, the Copa, the Diamond Horseshoe, and even Barbara Walters' father, Lou, who owned the Latin Quarter at the time. Ushers and ticket-takers at Madison Square Garden let him in for free and young Blye never missed a circus or a fight. On Saturday mornings, Swifty Morgan, the marginally successful gambler whom Damon Runyon often wrote about, would take Blye for English muffins and scrambled eggs at the Ham 'n' Eggery across the street where Swifty's ever-present bulldog, Jake, was served his scrambled eggs from a special plate on the floor. Sometimes, to pass the time, Irwin would sit in the radio cars of the *Daily News, Daily Mirror,* and *Journal-American,* which were always parked along West 51st Street, across from his father's store. Hunched in the back seat with jaded police reporters and photographers, Blye would listen to the various coded police calls squawking reports of ten-nines (fires), ten-thirties (stick-ups), and ten-ones (call your command and pick up the sandwiches).

"During the basketball-fixing scandal I remember the DA's office trailed my father around for two weeks until they decided that he wasn't a part of the point-shaving gang," Blye says.

"But Jack Molinas, who did get caught in that swindle, was a good customer and so were most of the ball players involved. In those days everybody used to buy their clothes in the Blye Shop. If you wanted a two-inch Billy Eckstine collar you had to go to Broadway. There weren't any stores out in the suburbs then. There were hardly any suburbs."

By twelve Blye had been pretty well stripped of illusions. He remembers uniformed cops from the Broadway beat leaving packages in the rear of his father's store. He had instructions never to touch those packages because they belonged to the cops. It didn't take Blye long to realize that the cops were using his father's store as a drop in which to store the loot they picked up from the merchants on their beats. He also learned that the reason they left their loot in the rear of the Blye Shop was that if they took it to their precinct lockers, the desk officers would insist on a cut or their fellow officers would steal it right out of the locker. It was safer at the Blye Shop than in the precinct.

Blye understood more about the nature of crooked cops at twelve than the Law Enforcement Assistance Administration could have ever taught him. Blye knew that the same mounted squad cop who let him ride the sixteen-hand bay, Murphy, along the narrow alleyways that separate the Broadway theaters, used to roll drunks he found sleeping off hangovers in those alleys. He remembers waiting one day while a detective friend of his father's who had promised to slip him into the Garden for the circus finished up a crap game on the second floor of the West 54th Street precinct. Suddenly, in the middle of the squad floor everything went still. Eight beefy detectives were hunched over their fists holding cash, their eyes riveted in disbelief on the sight of three dice on the floor instead of two. Before the first fist flew, young Blye was running down the precinct stairs back to his father's store. He was already too smart to want to be a witness. There would be no circus that day.

Despite the success of the Blye Shops (there were others dotted around the city), Irwin's father was usually broke. He remembers moving with his mother Minnie and father and sister Phyllis out of one apartment after another during his youth in order to avoid paying the rent.

"We rent-skipped like many others because we were broke," Blye says, "but that also meant that I went to a number of different schools in the Bronx alone."

School never interested Irwin. His father and mother insisted that an education was the only thing that would get Irwin out of the poverty cycle and had even saved some money in order to send Irwin to college when the time came. Irwin, however, found school far too dull when compared with the life he led on Broadway. How could he think about history when his Uncle Paul had promised to take him to the Luxor Baths that night for a "steam and a rub"? Blye remembers sitting in the steamroom of the West 46th Street club while his uncle talked with union delegates and racketeers.

"My Uncle Paul was a gangster buff," Blye says. "He enjoyed their company and liked knowing what was going on. I liked it too, but it made school pretty dull in the morning."

By the time he was fourteen, Irwin Blye wanted to be an actor. He liked the lifestyle. He loved the idea of being someone else all the time, of getting into different characters, of being applauded, of walking into stores, like Tony Martin, and ordering silk shirts, "three in each color."

Through the intervention of neighborhood friends Irwin Blye became the youngest student to study acting with Betty Cashman. In his class at the time were actors such as Bruce Gordon, who later played Frank Nitti in "The Untouchables" series, and Eric Flemming, who starred in "Rawhide," another TV series. At sixteen Blye was getting small parts in summer stock. In Greenwich, Connecticut, he played a newspaper reporter in *Golden Boy,* which starred John Garfield. He played the newspaper delivery boy in Tennessee Williams's *A Streetcar Named Desire* and got walk-on spots in the NBC-TV production of "The Greatest Story Ever Told."

"I had a beard and a robe," Blye says. "Only my mother knew it was me."

The only way Blye's father could convince him to go on to college after he graduated from high school was to stress the theater courses at Hofstra College.

"Within a year I thought I was going to go crazy," Blye says.

"One day I got so bored that instead of going to school I decided to spend the day with a friend of mine, Miles Asnas, on his job. He was an investigator for an insurance company. His uncle, Max Asnas, owned the Stage Deli on Seventh Avenue, and we both grew up around the midtown area although he's a little older than I am. He was an investigator checking negligence complaints for the Hartford Insurance Company at the time. I don't remember what we did that first day, but I remember how I felt when it was all over. That was what I wanted to do. I began going around with him a lot and finally I just gave up school completely. It broke my father's heart, but I had found something I really wanted to do and I was happy."

Blye dropped out of Hofstra before the year was over and applied for a job as an insurance investigator. The only problem, aside from the fact that it broke his father's heart, was that the insurance companies all insisted that applicants as investigators be college graduates. Blye was a college dropout, but he was already clever enough to finesse that sort of bureaucratic problem. Blye knew, for instance, that Hofstra would not release the records of their graduating students, or any of their students, to prospective employers unless the student had paid all his outstanding school fees. It was a strict school policy.

"It was perfect," Blye says. "The school sent everybody the same form letter—whether you were about to graduate with honors or had spent six months in the cafeteria, like me. It is the bureaucrat's idea of fairness. They'd send a letter to your employer saying they couldn't forward your record until you had paid up certain school fees. They'd also send a copy of the letter to you as a gentle reminder to pay up.

"Well, the first thing I did was get me a $5 library fee and made sure it was on my record," Blye continues. "And once I had that outstanding fee there was no way in the world that I was going to pay it. Because, from that moment on, all of the insurance companies that asked for my record from the school were told that it would not be forwarded until after I paid up. But insurance company personnel processors, and that's all personnel departments are, needed names to hire at that time. The insurance company, therefore, said that they would hire me on a temporary basis pending the payment of my school fees and their receiving my college transcript.

"Once I was hired," Blye says, "I was hired. As long as I did a decent job nobody was going to run around looking at whether or not I paid my library fee. The school didn't care, since they hadn't forwarded anything to anybody and wouldn't until I paid up. It was a little thing, but I saw a lot of things in it. I saw that the insurance company wasn't investigating its own employees very hard. I saw that the red tape and little bits of duplicate and triplicate papers always had angles to them that could be worked. I realized that once the red tape and the bureaucracy replaced a person who could look you right in the eye and ask a direct question, then you could fool the paper. Or, even better, figure out ways to use the paper, manipulate the red tape and bureaucracy to suit your own purposes.

"After three years with the insurance company," Blye continues, "I had enough experience, according to New York State law, to apply for a private investigator's license on my own. Until then I had worked as an assistant investigator attached to the officially licensed agent who worked for the insurance company. The license is issued by the New York Department of State and they give an examination once or twice a year. It wasn't very hard in those days. Lots of multiple choice stuff such as, 'If you find a body with a round hole in the head do you (a) go through the pockets (b) call the health department (c) call the police?'

"I was a cocky kid of twenty-five when I took the test," Blye says, "and the old political appointees who worked for the secretary of state weren't too sharp. The secretary of state at the time, by the way, was Carmine DeSapio. I finished the test early and looked around. Nobody else was moving. Most of the men taking the test were gray-haired ex-cops and they were still licking their pencil points and pondering over the first page.

"To make sure I wasn't too fast, I began to add up the questions and the points given for each to make sure that I hadn't missed any pages and forgotten to answer some of the questions. The test, we were told at the outset, was to add up to one hundred, but when I added it up I could only get ninety-four. I counted all the questions again. Ninety-four. I picked up the exam and went up to the

State Department official who was presiding. He was annoyed. He was afraid I was going to ask him something. I said I counted up the questions and they don't add up to one hundred like he said, but only to ninety-four. The guy was really annoyed at that. He began counting the questions and his finger shook so much with alcohol and palsy that he kept losing his place. Finally, he called another official over to add up the numbers. That guy added them up. Ninety-four.

" 'You finished with the test?' the second guy asks me after adding up the questions.

" 'Yes,' I said, like a dummy, thinking he was going to give me a medal.

" 'Then get the hell out of here and stop busting our chops,' the guy said, not only uninterested in the flaw in the test that I had told him about, but annoyed that I had done it. I walked out of that place feeling like the cat that brought the dead rat to the dinner table. I haven't volunteered as much since then."

11 **P**atty, the diminutive barmaid who might have the key to Tiny's freedom, lived in a small, white, one-family frame house on an icy suburban street. Many of the frozen front yards were littered with rusting tricycles and toppled hibachis. It was a quiet, sullen block, grimly awaiting spring. The perky door chime at Patty's house made Blye laugh.

The door opened a crack.

"Hello? My name is Irwin Blye. Is Patty here?"

Without a word the door opened to let Blye enter. It took a few seconds for his eyes to accustom themselves to the darkness inside, but finally he saw, not the barmaid he had expected, but at least a half dozen ghost figures in long grayish nightgowns. They stood around the room facing in different directions.

"I'm Irwin Blye. I'm looking for Patty. Is this her address?" Blye repeated dumbly, as he took in the astounding scene.

The wraithlike figures were elderly women. Their long, thinning gray hair had been tied off in scrawny bits with colored ribbons. They moved about the darkened room in slow motion carrying small bowls of breakfast cereal before them reverentially like vestal virgins in a grade B thriller.

Blye was transfixed.

"Come on in," a young, sprightly voice suddenly called out. "I'll be right with ya. Here! Here! In the back. Hi ya! Yeah, go through the kitchen. I'm near the basement steps. I just heard ya. I was taking a shower. Hi ya! Hi ya!"

It was Patty. She had been drying her close-cropped hair in a blue towel, and as Blye approached she turned around and led him down the basement stairs.

"I rent the basement," she explained. "The landlady makes extra money taking care of the retarded, but they never come down here. We can talk down here. It's like my own little home."

Patty was only four feet ten inches tall and weighed at least 170 pounds. But she was also surprisingly muscular. As she moved down the stairs toward the basement her hips stuck out from her waist almost like a shelf and her back and arms were hard, thick, and broad. When she turned around to look at Blye he was struck by the sweet, almost childlike face, but it came straight out of the neck and shoulders of a heavyweight wrestler.

"Helen called and told me what you wanted. She said that you were trying to help Tiny. Well, anything that I can do, you let me know. First, I know it couldn't have been Tiny who kidnapped the girl."

"How?" Blye asked.

"Because Tiny could have never gotten into the rear of a car. He couldn't fit in the rear of a car. He couldn't get into the rear of my car. Did you see it outside? It's not small. There was no way that Tiny could have been in the rear of that car with a girl in there with him. They just wouldn't fit. You could measure them."

As Patty spoke Irwin Blye made the kinds of mental notes private detectives rarely make in fiction. First he looked to see if she would be a credible witness on Tiny's behalf. Did she exude honesty, reliability, and the kinds of things that a South Carolina jury looked for in witnesses? It was never enough that the private detective find the alibi, he also had to find a source for that alibi that could pass muster with a jury and remain intact after being clawed over by the prosecution. Certainly, if the prosecutor ever got a look at her basement apartment it would not be too difficult to whittle away at her credibility. There was not an inch of shelf or floor space that was not filled with stuffed dolls and toys—a huge stuffed red panda, black and white poodles, rabbits, a pink Snoopy, almost as big as Patty, a green Mickey Mouse, and many monkeys.

"I love stuffed animals," Patty said when she noticed

Blye staring at the decor. "They're a weakness of mine."

Patty was seated primly on a green leatherette sofa, her feet barely touching a bright red shag rug. To her left was a silver Christmas tree. Eddie Arnold records were stacked in a wire metal record case, as was a $4.79 bargain David Cassidy record. Around her were a plaster gorilla with a banana, Raggedy Ann and Raggedy Andy dolls, a wastepaper basket with a yellow "Smile" face, red votive candles with figurines of saints, Chinese coolie dolls, and a framed, tinted print of her parents' wedding picture.

"I like stuffed animals because they remind me of the opposite sex. Tiny gave me the panda. He was always giving me something like that from the carnival. Most of the guys worked the rides and booths and they'd come to the bar after work and they knew I liked these dolls so they'd give them to me."

It was not long before Patty began spinning out a number of possible leads that might, indeed, prove that Tiny Berels was in New York on June 24. She said she knew he was there because they had had a party celebrating her father's birthday on that exact date.

"Tiny came over for a piece of cake," Patty said.

"Who else was there?" Blye asked.

"Gee, I don't remember right now."

"Try to remember, Patty. There must have been someone else at the party."

"Oh, sure there was, just give me a second."

"What about your father?" Blye asked.

"Oh, wait a minute. I know who can prove absolutely

that Tiny was here. Sure I can. I know exactly."

"Who, Patty?"

"Charlie O'Connell, that's who. Charlie might not want to talk about it, but he could give you the proof. I happen to know that Tiny used to live at Charlie's house. I know he was there until the end of June and every day in between. He gave me the big Snoopy at the end of June. Charlie is very suspicious, though. He might not want to talk because he's on welfare and he takes in boarders and if he admits that he had Tiny as a boarder he's afraid he'll lose his welfare money."

Charlie, Blye thought, must be the man identified as Charlie in Faucette's letter, the toothless alcoholic with whom Tiny said he lived while in Lake Ronkonkoma.

"Where does Charlie live?"

"I'll have to take you," Patty said. "I don't remember the exact address, but I know the house. I'll have to talk to him first, though. Besides worrying about the welfare, Charlie is mad at Tiny. He says Tiny owes him five dollars. When Tiny left Charlie screamed that Tiny still owed him the money. Charlie said that when Tiny came back he'd kill him."

"What about your father, Patty?" Blye pressed. "Can I talk to him?"

"My father died," Patty said, sadly.

"Oh, I'm sorry, Patty," Blye said, purposely lowering his voice to a properly funereal timbre. "How long ago did he die?"

"He died in October."

"You mean just two months ago?"

"No," Patty answered, "he died last October."

"Patty," Bly said, slowly, "if your father died the October before the last October how could he have had a birthday party last June? How could you and Tiny have celebrated his birthday if he was already dead?"

She looked blankly at Blye for a second.

"I know Tiny was at a party here. I thought it was my father's birthday party."

"Do you have your father's death certificate?" Blye asked.

"Oh, yeah," she said, "but I wish to Christ I knew what party it was. I thought it was Daddy's." And then, after a moment's pause, "Where the hell are my shoes?"

Driving with Patty to Charlie O'Connell's house she talked about how Tiny's arms were covered with tattoos and how, on one occasion, everyone in the bar stood around counting them. She also said that Tiny was not flabby, like Edna Moore had said, but solidly built.

"He did heavy work all the time," Patty said. "Once he even lifted the rear end of Charlie O'Connell's car out of the sand when it got stuck last summer."

The O'Connell house was a mess. Empty beer cans and bottles were sprinkled all over the lawn, along with broken aluminum sun chairs, gallon-size plastic detergent containers, and empty cans of cheap motor oil.

Patty jumped out of the car and bounced toward O'Connell's door, her calves flexing to the size of grapefruits with every step. The door opened and Patty went inside.

Blye just waited. It was nearly two o'clock in the afternoon. He had to see if he could get a statement out of Patty. Maybe O'Connell might be helpful. Helen had said she would try and reach Hale Richards, a twenty-one-year-old Lake Ronkonkoma boy who had worked with Tiny at the carnival and might be able to substantiate Tiny's alibi. Patty was too unreliable. It was obvious that she liked Tiny and she had said that she would be happy to go to North Carolina and testify on Tiny's behalf. However, despite the fact that she said she had never been arrested—a question asked of all prospective witnessess—and she said she had a married daughter and a son in the service, Blye felt she would make a terrible witness. Helen, the bar owner, would be good, but she could not pinpoint Tiny in Lake Ronkonkoma on the day in question. O'Connell might have a rent receipt or be able to say Tiny lived there for the month of June and hadn't been out of town on the twenty-fourth, but Patty had cautioned that he wouldn't be very cooperative. He was not only worried about losing his welfare check, but he was also a desperately sick alcoholic who sometimes saw rats and snakes.

"He'll talk to you," Patty said when she came out.

"Great," Blye said. "Where is he?"

"He'll meet you at the bar. He's got something to do first," Patty said, getting into Blye's car.

What is most startling to Irwin Blye, in his work on criminal cases, is the unrelieved chaos of the lives of the people involved. There are no Sydney Greenstreets wanting to talk to men who want to talk, nor are there any exotic females in black crepe snapping gold cigarette lighters with the wrong initials. That tidy world of calculation and plot is not real. What Irwin Blye sees is nothing but loose ends, wrong addresses, transposed telephone numbers, witnesses who turn out not to be witnesses, an army of walk-ons, terrified and ignorant of everything around them. The people involved in crimes are invariably poor. Grindingly poor. They are part-time people, like Patty and Tiny and Charlie. Their whole lives are spent on nothing but part-time jobs. They will never own a new car, they will never own an automobile in which everything—windshield wipers, heater, directionals, brake lights, and radio—all work at the same time.

Their lives, Blye says, are clouded in alcohol and fantasy. Their children have found grass and, sometimes, heroin. A week can be sustained by the thought of Friday night bowling, but the bowling party can disintegrate into a screaming match or brawl over an imagined slight, an accidental shove, or a dispute over who paid for the last round of beers. It is a frightening world barely able to contain its anger and very capable of using for vengeance the only weapon it has—violence.

"They sit there nice and quiet, looking at you from the corner of their eyes, and it dawns on them that your tie is making too much noise and what the hell are you doing in their house anyway. They begin to forget that you are working for their lawyer so that they can collect $1,200 for falling down the icy subway platform. You can begin to sense it, or you had better begin to sense it or get the hell out of the business. You can begin to see the way the guy puts down his glass, the way he looks away and mumbles curses under his breath, the way he yells at the dog or kids or sister-in-law or kicks the table leg, and then he's had it and he's got the breadknife in his hand or a fork or anything nearby, except the beer can or drink he's milking, and his wife yells and you get up from the table and she takes the knife away and gets mad at him and he sits down again, just as angry as before, but now he's shown he has some spunk. He's put the sonofabitch with the loud tie in his place, and then everything settles down as though nothing had happened. Daddy tried to carve up the man writing on the paper with the bread-knife, that's all.

"That is why I am very careful in dealing with poor people," Blye continues. "They don't have very much. They don't have anything, in fact. And all the feistiest ones have left is a sensitivity and concern for their own idea of personal dignity. These are the kinds of power-less people who take orders from somebody all their lives, use service elevators, wait on line, and know, by watching television every night, that they have been left out. They feel screwed and they can be very sensitive. Get them after working hours and they don't have to smile and kiss ass. I see them sitting on the stoops of their tenements drinking beer and they're changed peo-ple. The guy milking his beer who was all smiles and kissy-ass in the factory or delivering packages is now in his own domain. And if you think he's going to be the same as he was during working hours you're nuts. I move very carefully in this world. I think their unrelieved poverty and continuous lack of dignity have made them all a little mad. I mean crazy and angry. You ask a question wrong, you don't show enough respect to the man of the house, you look at his two-hundred-pound wife with what he thinks is horny intent, and it's fists and kicks and knives and guns and anything else that happens to be around. Then the cops come and the ambulance comes and they cart away the debris and within minutes there are other people exactly like them sitting on the same stoop.

"I learned long ago to avoid these kinds of problems by being elaborately polite in that kind of world," Blye goes on. "It's always mister and missus and thank you and pardon me and please and may I and I hate to bother you until they begin to feel as though you're not some wise sonofabitch looking to rip off the last thing they got, their dignity. It's amazing. Once these people see that you are showing them the same kind of consideration they've seen shown to big shots they become less wary, less antagonistic, and then you can begin the business at hand."

Hale Richards was waiting for Irwin Blye at the Good Time Bar. Hale, a local boy who had worked at jobs in the area since dropping out of school in his early teens, had worked in the carnival with Tiny through June and could swear that Tiny even hung around for four or five days after he was fired. That, put together with the information from Harry Fried, the carnival owner, that Tiny was fired on either the twenty-third, twenty-fourth, or twenty-fifth, could help establish the fact that Tiny was in New York at the time of the kidnapping.

Richards was tall and thin. His long, lanky brown hair hung over his forehead and ears. His wife, a small, pinch-faced girl with wire-thin lips, who was probably no more than eighteen, sat grimly beside her young husband. She rocked a baby whose clothes were badly stained and whose face was smudged. The child seemed as listless as the mother. A two-year-old was wandering around the bar picking up empty cigarette packs while some of the patrons slyly pelted him with peanuts.

"It was me," Hale began, "and Benny and Bill and Tiny, and we all worked together on the carnival from the day it came here until the end. I was on the Octopus and we worked seven days a week until it closed. I was there every morning till night and so was Tiny. We were like a family. We had some good times. One time we had a big barbecue right here, in back, and then we swam in the lake."

Hale looked at Helen for confirmation and she nodded in agreement.

"I remember Tiny was fired," Hale continued, "but I swear he was here about five days after the carnival closed. I remember, the day he was fired, we went to Bevins' Amusements in Port Jefferson looking for work. We picked up Tiny in the shopping center in front of Jack-in-the-Box. We had Lenny's Pontiac. There was me and Lenny and some girl and Tiny and Benny. They all got fired along with Tiny. But a guy at the carnival called the foreman at Bevins' Amusements and told him that Tiny and the rest of us had been fired, so we didn't get the jobs.

"I know the second night after he was fired I lent him ten dollars to go into Sophie's, the topless bar. I know he came back the next day—that's the third day after he was fired—and was in the bar here talking about the topless and joking."

"That's right," Patty interjected. "They were kidding with me about the topless and he was drinking his Jack Daniels and Tangerade."

"Fine," Blye said. "Have you ever been arrested, Hale?"

"Yes," Hale said, without any hesitation.

"What for?" Blye asked.

"Burglary."

"Were you convicted?"

"Yes."

Blye then began to dictate Hale's statement, line by line, and Hale nodded in agreement as Blye carefully pronounced the sentence he was writing.

On this 5th day of January 1975, I, Hale Richards, married, say that I am (21) twenty-one years of age and residing at 82 Hogart Street, Lake Ronkonkoma, Long Island, New York. This is a one family house with no telephone. I am at this address since February 1974. I am unemployed. My wife's first name is Maria. She is a housewife. I was employed by Carnival Amusements, Inc. I first started in East

Islip at the Great Eastern Store on Sunrise Highway. I started tearing down the sides three nights prior to going to Lake Ronkonkoma. I was working the Octopus ride with . . .

After Blye had taken Hale's statement he asked the young man to write in at the bottom of the page that he had read the two pages and forty-three lines and that he understood each and every line and that they were true.

Hale was a little hesitant.

When Blye looked over at Hale's scribblings he noticed that Hale had spelled the word "read" as "red" and "true" came out "tir." Blye then thanked Hale for his help, rewrote the paragraph about understanding every line and asked Hale to sign the page.

Charlie O'Connell was next. He was fifty-one years old, but looked as if he was in his late sixties. O'Connell had no teeth and a day-old stubble on a bony, crease-lined face. He was almost emaciated, and his brown trousers and plaid wool shirt billowed on his frame. His speech was slurred and almost unintelligible. At first he denied that Tiny had lived with him, but was prodded by those gathered around the table, including a fidgety youngster named Benny. Benny was the seventeen-year-old who had gone looking for the job at Bevins' after they had all been fired. Benny, it turned out, was Charlie O'Connell's son.

"He's not going to make any trouble," Helen finally said, trying to impress upon O'Connell that Blye was not a welfare inspector. "He's not from the county."

O'Connell finally relented and said that Tiny had moved in with him shortly after coming to Lake Ronkonkoma with the carnival.

"At first he slept in a truck and they used to bring him coffee," O'Connell said, pointing at Hale and Maria.

He said that he let Tiny stay at his house and that Tiny owed him money and Tiny owed everybody in town money. He said, as ominously as he could between the slurs, that there were people looking for Tiny. O'Connell agreed, however, that Tiny did not leave Lake Ronkonkoma until after June 24, but he could offer no proof of his certainty.

"Maybe Pennisi will know," Benny interjected. "I know Tiny ate there every day and paid at the end of the week. Maybe they'll know."

The Lakeside Luncheonette was within walking distance of the Good Time. It had a counter with fixed rotating stools and a row of tables and chairs against one wall. There was a grill for hamburgers and two deep-fat fryers for everything else. Coffee was served out of thick-lipped and very heavy cups, the kind with a hole in the handle too small to put the smallest finger through.

Dominick Pennisi was in his middle forties and had been scraping hamburgers off the grill for two years. He was perpetually angry and his anger was clearly visible in the contempt he showed for his clients. He never smiled. Every order given to him was as welcome as another bamboo split under a fingernail. It was nearly three o'clock in the afternoon and although the luncheon rush had long subsided, Pennisi still had not shaved. He was not pleased to see Irwin Blye. Blye had to explain several times exactly who he was and whom he represented. Once Pennisi was convinced that Blye was a real private detective he became a little more cooperative.

Yes, he said, Tiny was a regular customer of his. He had met Tiny at the carnival. Tiny was flabby around the neck and arms. He did not know why Blye asked that question. Tiny was as strong "as a bull." He thought Tiny might have left Lake Ronkonkoma sometime in June for a couple of days, but he couldn't say when. He also told Blye, rather cryptically, that after several conversations with Tiny, he was sure Tiny was capable of doing "many bad things."

"What, specifically?" Blye asked.

"Let me just say he was no angel," Pennisi added. "I know bad buys, you know bad guys, we know what we're talking about. Right? Do I have to say more? You get my meaning? You come in and tell me Tiny did a bad thing, I don't know if he did it, but I know he could have done it."

"Well," Blye asked, "maybe your records for June will show that he was here on the twenty-fourth. Maybe you've got him down on the tab for that day?"

Pennisi pulled out the grease-stained ledger and opened to June of 1975. He had written in Tiny's name, followed by $13.75 total owed, but there were no specific dates for the lunches Tiny had eaten. Another uncertainty. Blye didn't even bother to take a statement from Pennisi.

Benny O'Connell was waiting in Blye's car.

"I know Tiny was here," he insisted to Blye. "I was with him every day after he was fired. I saw him in my father's house every day. I can swear to that, even if my father is afraid."

Blye took Benny O'Connell's statement: "Tiny lived with my father from the date the carnival came to town, or maybe a day or two later, till he left. Tiny was in Lake Ronkonkoma till several days after the carnival closed."

It was now after three o'clock and Blye did not have much more time to search for Tiny's alibi. He took a picture of the Good Time Bar with Hale Richards, Patty, Benny, and Helen standing out front. He would recommend to Bob Faucette that Helen Mann would probably be the only witness in Lake Ronkonkoma worth flying down for Tiny's defense. But he wanted Faucette to see what the other potential witnesses looked like.

Richards' criminal record made him practically useless. Patty was so anxious to help Tiny that she was more than willing to lie and not lie very well. Her story about her father's birthday party with Tiny a year after her father was dead indicated to Blye that she could, at best, be easily confused. Benny O'Connell was okay. He could at least establish that Tiny stayed in the O'Connell house, but there was no proof of the specific day Tiny finally left. Charlie O'Connell was too far gone. Blye would also recommend that Harry Fried, the carnival owner, might make a presentable witness, as he could establish that Tiny was in New York on the twenty-third, twenty-fourth, or twenty-fifth. The rest of the witnesses all agreed that Tiny stayed around a couple of days after he was fired. Perhaps that, added to the discrepancies in the description, might be enough to give Tiny's North Carolina jurors reasonable doubts.

At no time during his entire investigation of Tiny's whereabouts on the day of June 24, 1975, did Irwin Blye think about the question of Tiny's innocence or guilt. Such thoughts get in the way. Looking for the kinds of puzzle pieces needed by defense attorneys does not leave much room for idle speculation. There was enough doubt about Tiny actually being in North Carolina on the June 24th date to make Blye think that perhaps Tiny was telling the truth. The description and the six-month period between the kidnapping and the arrest and identification also gave Blye a moment's pause. And then there was the way Tiny was insisting that he was innocent. He was facing a stiff term by going before a jury on a kidnapping charge. If he had copped a plea and implicated the other two men in the car with him—providing that he was the kidnapper—his own charges would have been reduced. But then, maybe the deal he was offered by the prosecutor was not good enough for such a deal. After all, the prosecutor had the victim herself willing to identify Tiny smack there in the middle of the court. A pretty little girl who, according to Bob Faucette, looked like she stepped out of a Billy Graham rally, pointing her little finger at that big ol' fat carnival worker. What woman on the jury would want to run up against that fat man in a dark alley at night?

It was just before Blye left the Good Time Bar, after explaining to all the potential witnesses that they might

be called to testify on Tiny's behalf, that Benny let drop
the one remark of the day that caught Blye's attention.
Blye had finished taking everyone's statement and all of
the ball-points had been put away. The various people
who had given their bits of information to Blye were now
comparing notes with each other over beers. Business
was picking up and Helen began helping behind the bar.
Charlie O'Connell felt that he had weathered a tremendous interrogation and was looking slyly at Blye and
laughing heartily with his pals whom he had joined at the
bar. Hale and his wife were excited. Benny was jumping
up and down. The jukebox was playing Stevie Wonder.
Blye's visit was almost over and it had broken up the
monotony of their lives. Now they didn't want him to
leave. All around the bar they began retelling their tales.
Benny and Hale were talking about their trip with Tiny
in Lenny's car the day they got fired. They joked about
how they hardly made it.

"Why?" Blye asked, heading for the door and the
other cases he had yet to work that day.

"It was in bad shape," Benny said. "Lenny had a loud
car. It made a lot of noise."

Smiling and waving goodbye, Blye drove out of Lake
Ronkonkoma. Before getting on the Long Island Expressway and returning to the city where he still had to
talk with a divorce-minded doctor's wife and a tenant of
a slum building who had a negligence case against the
city, Blye pulled over to the side of the road. He began
thumbing through the papers that had been sent him by
Bob Faucette, looking for the FBI report of the state-

ment taken from Edna Moore shortly after she had been
kidnapped.

The automobile's muffler was broken making a
loud roaring noise, leaking fumes into the passen-
ger section, and the upholstery was a brownish gray,
not fabric. The noise made overhearing conversation difficult.

It proved nothing, of course. Noisy mufflers were not
rare. But it did offer the possibility that Tiny and Lenny
and Hale (Benny did not fit the description of the other
two men Edna Moore identified) could have gone on a
trip south in Lenny's noisy car shortly after they had
been fired. They could have driven south right after they
had been turned down for a job at Bevins'. Patty's recol-
lection that they all returned to the bar the next day and
talked about Tiny going to the topless could be Patty's
faulty memory again. It was all speculation but the remark about the noisy car came down heavily against Tiny
as far as Blye's private feelings were concerned.

12 "It's the bullshit that bothers me most," Irwin Blye said. He was driving west along the Long Island Expressway toward New York. He still had the doctor's wife from Hartsdale and the scalded woman in the South Bronx to interview.

"This is really a job that requires professionals. It's not enough anymore to muscle your way around or rely on some old buddies with whom you once pounded the beat. It's all gotten much more complicated than that. The guy who expects to survive and prosper in the business had better look upon it as a profession and not as a retirement plan.

"I can understand those people who have never had to

use a private detective having no idea of who or what they are, but I've found even professionals who should know better are out on a limb. They really think it's still cowboy days when a private would swear to anything and hope it works out in court. There are lots of lawyers so anxious to win a case that if the private wants their business he'd better be prepared to lie and then take the heat if it blows up in his face. That's the price some lawyers demand if you want to work for them.

"I had a beautiful example of that just a few weeks ago. It had to do with a big Boston bank wanting to serve papers on a New Jersey builder. The builder, a guy by the name of Kayser, and the bank had been part of a 70-million-dollar deal that collapsed. The builder had put up $5 million of his own money in notes to guarantee his end.

"Once the deal fell apart the bank began to call in all the chips, and one of the chips they called in was the New Jersey builder and his $5 million worth. This entailed the bank employing a New Jersey lawyer and serving the builder with papers alerting him to the fact that the bank wanted the $5 million he had promised in case the deal fell through.

"The bank went to a power-packed New Jersey law firm and the head of the firm gave the case to the eagerest beaver in the firm. The firm obviously wanted to show the big bucks from Boston what a terrific firm they were so they turned it over to Mister Aggressive. The bank wanted the builder served with papers so they could get him into court and get his $5 million in default. The man lived in a very upper income area and it would require identifying the man and serving him or his wife personally with the papers.

"The law firm worked with a New York lawyer who I had often done business with, and when they asked him for the name of a private investigator who could help the local sheriff to serve papers on a New Jersey builder, I was recommended. In New Jersey out-of-state investigators can't serve papers. It was a recommendation I could have done without. First, when I meet with the eager-beaver lawyer I realize that he wants the papers served as soon as possible and he doesn't really care how it is done. I tell him we'll have to put the man's house under surveillance in order to know when he's home. There's no point in serving the wrong man or woman. The lawyer laughed. He thought it was a joke.

"The bank that wanted the man served had a business address for him in Florida and a home address for him in Oakland, New Jersey. The next Sunday after taking the assignment I got Herta and the children and piled them all into Herta's car, a two-year-old red Caddy, and drove over to Jersey. I'll often use Herta and the kids as a cover. They're perfect. Herta, of course, knows what we're doing, but the kids usually think it's another boring ride into the country and can be relied upon to jump up and down in the rear of the car, making the cover even better.

"The house was at the top of a long hill and right away I knew that it had been built with security in mind. Builders and real estate people are forever getting served with papers in one kind of civil action or another and they usually learn to be very cautious. This Jersey builder was going to be no exception. The house was set off from the road, which ended in a cul de sac. It had other houses on either side and there was a fourth house across the cul de sac, but that was it. The top of the hill. In order to get into the builder's house you had to leave the car in the cul de sac and walk down a narrow path that had been cleared of any shrubbery or trees that might block the owner's vision of who was coming to dinner. The path led straight to a small footbridge that crossed over a Japanese garden. On the other side of the bridge there was a white wooden picket fence with a speaker box attached to the post nearest the gate. There was no lock on the gate.

"The house looked like a one-story building in front, but in the rear, on the sloping side of the hill, it was actually three stories high and had a three-car garage tucked underneath. From the front the house looked like a South Bronx supermarket. Burglar-proof and ugly. There was nothing you could see. There was a row of high, narrow windows running just below the slightly peaked roofline, but curtains covered those windows pretty well. There was one large oak door that looked like it weighed several hundred pounds, and there were two long narrow panels of very thick, shatterproof glass on either side of the door frame.

"With Herta looking down from the car in the street, and the kids jumping up and down and squealing, I spoke into the speaker box at the gate. There was no answer. I spoke into it again. Still no answer. That was okay. I then went across the street to a young fellow who was shooting baskets against the garage door. I told him I was looking for a Mr. Gerald. He sees me and he sees Herta and the Caddy and the kids and I know he feels sorry for me right away. He doesn't know any Mr. Gerald he says. That doesn't surprise me since I took the Gerald name off a roadside mailbox driving up the hill. That's weird, I tell him, feigning ignorance. The address I have for Gerald is the address across the street and there doesn't seem to be anyone home.

" 'No!' he tells me. 'That's the Kayser house.'

" 'Maybe it's Mr. Kayser I want,' I say.

" 'I haven't seen him for a while,' the basketball player says, 'but maybe Mrs. Kayser is home.'

"We go back and forth like this for a few minutes and I find that Kayser lives there with his wife and two children and a maid.

"The reason I wanted to know as much as I could about the man I had to serve was to avoid serving the wrong person. If someone had answered the Kayser door, for instance, I would have glanced back at Herta and the kids squealing in the car and said that I was supposed to meet a Mr. Smith or Gerald or whoever at this address. Even subpoena-shy people are usually helpful to a man with a wife and kids. I ask if I could borrow their telephone directory. I'll try to get the most out of my view of the inside of the house. You want to see who the maid is, if there's a sister-in-law or somebody's mother visiting. Also, when you finally go to court to swear that the summons was lawfully served it helps to be able to say 'I was there on such and such a day and this person identified herself as Mrs. Kayser and this one as Mrs. Kayser's maid or mother or whoever.

"The next day I called the eager-beaver attorney and said that it looked like Mr. Kayser might be away, but Mrs. Kayser was probably living there. I suggested we put a surveillance on the house. Get to see who went in and out of the house. A surveillance, by the way, does not mean getting dressed up like a telephone repairman and sitting on a pole near the Kayser driveway. Ninety-nine per cent of the surveillances made, incidentally, take place from your car. I drove up the cul de sac the next morning a little before 7 A.M. in my own car and pulled off the side of the road so I wouldn't block anyone. I didn't try to hide my car or disguise it in any way. I was just a man in an automobile parked off the road on the top of a hill near a cul de sac somewhere in New Jersey.

"In places like Kings Point, Long Island, you can last about ten minutes doing that before the police arrive and want to know what you're doing there. In New Jersey I sat on a surveillance outside the Kayser house for two days and no one ever bothered me.

"You need a couple of things on a good surveillance. A pair of binoculars help. I use a lightweight pair of Japanese-make 8 x 24s. You don't need much more than that, you're not looking for U-boats. Then you need an empty container to pee in since chances are you won't be able to find any rest rooms where you are planted. Many a good plant has been lost for want of a men's room.

"I watched the place for two days and never saw a thing. Nobody went in and nobody ever left. The law firm didn't want a twenty-four-hour surveillance. If they did, I would have brought somebody else on the case with me. They only wanted surveillance from around 7 A.M. until 9 P.M.

"On the third day I was thinking that this job was getting a little boring when I pulled into my regular spot and noticed that there was an air-conditioning truck parked near the garage. Now I knew somebody was home. I got out of my car and walked down the path. I opened the gate and went right to the door. I rang the bell and waited.

"A woman came to the door. She had auburn hair, brown eyes, was very nicely dressed, and appeared to be in her mid-thirties. She was also carrying a dust rag.

" 'Is Mr. Kayser home?' I asked.

" 'No,' she says, very curt.

"Now I know immediately that she's suspicious. I can sense it. She was not nasty, but not quite polite. She was hard. That's the way to describe her. Hard.

" 'Are you Mrs. Kayser?' I ask.

" 'No,' she says.

" 'I'd like to speak to them,' I say.

" 'He's out of town and she's out,' is the reply.

" 'Well,' I said, 'I would like them to call me when they get in,' and I give her my name and number.

"I called the lawyer right after I left the house and he nearly jumped out of his skin. 'You got him!' he kept shouting, 'You got him!'

"I kept telling him that it was a woman and that the woman denied that she was Mrs. Kayser.

" 'It doesn't matter in New Jersey,' he says. 'If we serve the wife it's like serving the husband.'

" 'I'm not even sure it's the wife,' I say; 'it could be the maid.'

" 'Describe her,' he says, and I do, right from the phone booth off the main road. Meanwhile, he gets the county sheriff on the other line and alerts him to the fact that he might be able to serve the papers on Mrs. Kayser. The sheriff is anxious to do the job, because the firm has promised him $50. The lawyer tells the sheriff my description of the woman who answered the Kayser door and then he jumps back into my ear.

" 'That's her,' the guy shrieks. 'The sheriff says the description fits. He served her before on some other matter. It was minor. Where are you now? We'll meet you and then go over to the house and serve the papers.'

"I told him where I was and in a few moments the lawyer comes squealing into the parking area near the phone booth with the sheriff following in his car. They fling open their doors and come charging out toward me. You'd think they were getting ready for a gunfight instead of just serving some damn papers for a civil court action. Anyway, I tell them what I know and I can see they are both going bananas with excitement. The sheriff, by the way, is not anybody in a cowboy hat and spurs. The sheriff is the official title given to court officers in civil suits and they wear regular businessmen's clothes.

It's the sheriff, for instance, who dispossesses people who don't pay their rent. In New Jersey it's the sheriff who serves legal papers on people like Mr. or Mrs. Kayser.

"We drive up to the dead end in two cars. The lawyer and I stand at the top of the drive and watch the sheriff go toward the white picket fence. Instead of going through the fence, however, the guy stops and says something into the voice box. Then, instead of going through the gate to the door he sticks the legal papers between two of the spokes on the picket fence and joins us on the top of the hill.

"I didn't say anything, but the lawyer asked, 'Did you serve her?'

" 'Yes,' the sheriff said. 'She identified herself and she took the service.'

"It was still none of my business so I didn't say anything, except now I knew something about the way this young eager lawyer was willing to operate. I also knew that if I ever had a defendant who had been served in New Jersey I probably should look very closely to make sure that the service was legal. This time I was on the other side, however, so it didn't matter.

"About a week later I get a call from the lawyer. He says they were making up the affidavit about the serving of the legal papers on Mrs. Kayser and the sheriff had signed that he had served them on her and they wanted me to sign that I had seen her accept the papers.

" 'Bob,' I said to the poor guy, 'I didn't see that.'

" 'Well, I saw it,' he says.

" 'Well, you may have seen it,' I say, 'but I'm afraid I didn't.'

" 'I'll get back to you,' he says. He was always getting back to me. He checked everything with his big boss and the boss was apparently very anxious to please the bank and the young lawyer was very anxious to please his boss. It was one of those things where everybody leans over just a little more than they should to please somebody. It's the domino theory of pleasing people and a terrific way to get in a lot of trouble. The big boss lawyer, for instance, he's insulated from trouble. He wants everything done perfect. He didn't authorize any shortcuts. The anxious lawyer isn't telling anyone to say what they didn't see. The fact that he claims to have seen what he says he saw should be hint enough of what he wants. The sheriff will swear to anything for $50 and probably 50 per cent of the papers he serves are either left in the milk box or thrown away.

"Within a few minutes the lawyer calls me back.

" 'It's okay,' the lawyer tells me, 'we've drawn up the affidavit that the sheriff identified himself and Mrs. Kayser identified herself and she accepted the service from the sheriff through a slot in the door.'

" 'Bob,' I said to the guy as gently as I could, 'that door is solid oak. There's no mail slot or slot of any kind.'

" 'I'll get back to you,' he says.

"Couple of hours later he calls. 'We've written up the affidavit that says she identified herself and we left the papers there.'

" 'What happened to the mail slot?' I asked.

(*176*)

" 'That was a mistake,' he answered, hardly missing a beat.

"Had they signed that affidavit with the mail slot the sheriff and the law firm would have been dead. Kayser's lawyer would have stayed nice and quiet until the first court appearance and then supplied the court with the picture of the front door proving that there was no mail slot and accusing the sheriff and the bank's law firm of an improper service of papers. Everyone would have been back to step one, do not pass go, do not collect $200.

"I didn't say anything.

" 'You're not going to make me unhappy with you, are you?' the young lawyer finally says.

"I told him that I would try not to make him unhappy, but all I could say was that a woman, who I could describe, had answered the door earlier. The sheriff could then say anything he wanted and he would apparently identify Mrs. Kayser from the description I gave and the fact that he had previously served her with a subpoena. The business about whether he had actually served Mrs. Kayser or not didn't matter; they were apparently going to brazen it out. It was the word of the sheriff and the lawyer against the word of the woman. They would have liked to add my name to the affidavit, but they didn't need it.

" 'Remember the air-conditioning truck?' I finally asked the lawyer.

" 'Yeah,' he said.

" 'Well, maybe the repairman can tell us if Mrs. Kayser was the woman who was home.'

" 'Terrific,' he says, 'let me get back to you.'

"A few minutes later he's back on the phone. 'Go to it,' he says.

" 'This can backfire,' I tell him. "If the repairman is a guy who does a lot of business with them he could take their side or tip them to the fact that we need cooperation in the service.'

" 'I'll get back to you.'

" 'Go get 'em,' he said, after talking to his boss.

"I had written the name of the air-conditioning company down in my pad, along with his address and telephone number. I had also written down the license plates of cars that had passed by during the two days I sat on surveillance outside the house. Every couple of hours I'd note down license plate numbers, clearly identifying the plate numbers and make of the car with the time and date.

"It helps in establishing that you have been on the surveillance for the court and that the chances are that the papers were properly served. Anyway, I called the repairman and went over to see him. It turned out he didn't give much of a damn one way or the other. The man was beautiful. He had the most detailed set of books you could imagine. He had every call made to the company and every day he was out. On the day I saw him in the Kayser driveway he had been working in the house. He was there from seven until noon. He had been let in through the door in the rear and the maid had let him in.

"I asked him if he meant the woman who had opened

the door for me that day, describing for him the well-dressed auburn-haired woman holding the dust cloth.

" 'Yeah,' he said, 'that's her. That's the maid.'

" 'Where was Mrs. Kayser?' I asked.

" 'Mrs. Kayser wasn't home that day,' he says.

"When I call back the lawyer and tell him this he's really in a fit. They have already filed the affidavit with the court and now he wants to know from me how he can get out of the fix. The bank apparently thinks that Kayser has been legitimately served. The law firm, anxious for the bank's New Jersey business, doesn't tell them anything that isn't good news and so the eager beaver is sitting there holding the bag. I had told him to wait before serving the paper. His firm, by the way, was getting a huge fee from the bank to handle this little transaction for them. I was paid $500 for the surveillance and the sheriff got a big $50 for screwing up the service. The bank, meanwhile, stood to lose Kayser's $5 million guarantee because of this screwup. All I could tell eager beaver was to sit tight and see what happened.

"Within ten days it happened. Mr. Kayser's attorneys said their client was never legally served. They said that the court papers were served on the wrong person. It was a real mess. In the meantime, the lawyer had checked and found that in New Jersey a husband, wife, *or* live-in maid could be served with legal papers. That meant that they could have served the woman who opened the door for me and been perfectly legit. Instead they concocted this elaborate story about serving Mrs. Kayser. And the Kayser attorneys, knowing that the live-in maid was home at

the time we were there, didn't want to say she was present because that would have meant service was possible.
They just took our lie and threw another lie right back
at us, saying that we served a child with the papers.

"Are you beginning to get an idea about the legal
profession? You get the way it works? The sheriff meanwhile wasn't a 100 per cent liar. He had actually served
a summons on the Kayser maid on an earlier occasion,
but she had said or made him believe that she was Mrs.
Kayser, so that poor dumbo actually thought that Mrs.
Kayser was somewhere in the house as far as my description was concerned.

" 'You've got to start from the beginning,' I told the
young lawyer. 'You've got to establish a new surveillance
and get them with a nail and mail. You've got to establish
that the Kaysers are actually trying to avoid the service
of court papers. Call the local police and establish with
them that you are on a surveillance outside the Kayser
house in order to serve legal papers. You must do that
every eight hours for a week. You've got to note down
the license plates of cars that pass by during the week and
note the exact date and time. You've got to begin dropping in on neighbors and introducing yourself and establishing your presence. If the situation should come to it
you would be able to subpoena these people and establish that you were outside the Kayser house for a pro-
longed period of time.

" 'You then have got to try and actually serve the summons several times. Three, four—or even five. And then
finally, after you have established that you've been trying

to serve the papers and that the Kaysers, or whoever, have been trying to avoid it, you nail or pin a copy of the court papers to the house door and certify-mail a copy of the papers to prove that it was delivered to the right address.'

"That's where the lawyers for the bank are now. He said he'd get back to me. I had a message that he had called this morning, but I haven't had a chance to call him back."

13

Mrs. Nancy Stein lived in a large rambling house on a tree-lined street in Hartsdale. She and her doctor husband, Robert, had raised their three children there over the last twenty-two years and now they were separated. He had been living in an apartment near the hospital that had been taking up more and more of his time for several years, and she had been spending more and more time rattling around alone in the eleven-room house. First to go was the oldest son, Charles, who was now twenty and living at Harvard. Then Gail, nineteen, decided she wanted to go to Radcliffe. Now, with her husband living in an apartment near the hospital, Mrs. Stein was alone in the house with Meryl, fourteen, who was still a freshman at the local high school.

The bell had not finished ringing before Mrs. Stein had the door open. It was a big, comfortable house. Floor lamps with amber shades cast a disarming mellowness throughout the first floor. There was nothing mellow about Mrs. Stein, however. She stood there with one hand on the door, squinting out nervously from behind a curtain of cigarette smoke. She was suspicious. Irwin Blye had been recommended to her by her attorney and she had checked him out with several other attorneys, as well. When he introduced himself, the first thing she asked for was his identification. She looked at it carefully and then invited him into the parlor.

Mrs. Stein had not been getting much sleep. She had more creases in her face than a woman in her mid-forties should have. Family photographs of happier days showed that she had gained at least thirty pounds since the separation a year earlier. This day she was wearing a pair of loose-fitting gray flannel slacks and a navy crewneck sweater over an open-collared pink shirt. She moved about the house in swift, jerky movements. It was obvious that the impending divorce and the settlement had become the most important thing in her life. Her house had been turned over to the battle. The dining room table, for instance, was stacked high with neatly tied batches of folders. At one end, Mrs. Stein had arranged her typewriter, an adding machine, and several Dundee marmalade jars filled with pencils and ball-point pens.

Motioning Blye toward a couch in the living room,

Mrs. Stein flicked her ashless cigarette in the direction of one of the tiny ashtrays that dotted the house.

"Meryl! Mer!" Mrs. Stein called out, craning her neck to be heard at the top of the stairs. "Mer, give us some warning if you're coming down."

Mrs. Stein then began talking very rapidly at Blye, and loudly enough to be heard everywhere in the house. She asked Blye if he wanted some mulled wine, said that she had spoken to several attorneys and that they all said he made a "nice appearance," and added that she was going about the divorce matter as carefully as possible. She suspected her husband was trying to hide some of his assets from her so that he could beat her out of her rightful share of their total holdings. As Mrs. Stein spoke she kept toying with the eyeglasses that she wore strung around her neck like pearls.

"You want to know about the bank books first?" Mrs. Stein began, looking straight at Blye, trying very hard to be open with a man who had just walked in her door.

"That's a good place to start," Blye answered, assuming the tone and role of a doctor routinely going through a patient's various symptoms.

As Mrs. Stein began enumerating her husband's holdings, she also included how badly he had treated her during their marriage. She spoke, Blye thought, in a clear, ringing tone that was intended to be heard by her fourteen-year-old daughter at the top of the stairs. It did not surprise him. Private detectives, even more than the divorce lawyers themselves, are often used as a vehicle for vengeance by the people who hire them.

"You become *their* detective," Blye explains. "They are going to get even with the person they are divorcing and the private detective is a perfect sounding board. What Mrs. Stein was after, though, was more than just vengeance. You learn to read between the lines, and it always happens in divorces involving doctors. The wives don't want to come right out and say it, but what all of this is about is Mrs. Stein is trying to get me to find her husband's hidden assets. Judging from the tremendous amount of divorce work I've done with doctors' wives, just about every doctor in the country must be gypping the income tax people. That's what Mrs. Stein really wanted me to find out. That's what all the doctors' wives want. They know that their husbands pocket a quarter or two-thirds of their incomes in cash. They went on those vacations to Hawaii where they even paid for the airline tickets in cash. Now that the honeymoon and marriage are over, the doctor's wife wants that illegal income somehow worked out in the settlement.

"What men like me are supposed to do," Blye continues, "is get enough on the husband as far as holding out on Uncle Sam is concerned so that his wife and her lawyer can go to work on him and get a nice buy-off price. None of it showing on paper, of course, just everybody working with tax-free dollars that the good old doctor has been salting away. I've done so many of these cases and so many of the doctors do not report a portion of their incomes on their tax returns that I think they must have a class in tax-dodging at most American medical colleges."

It was an easy job as far as Irwin Blye was concerned.
Mrs. Stein had detailed information about all of her husband's sources of income. She had joint income tax returns they had filed when they were living together. She
hinted that she was certain her husband made much
more than he reported on his income tax return and it
was part of his untaxed income she wanted. She suggested that he saw private patients on Tuesdays and
Thursdays and that he usually pocketed the cash from
these patients. She said his mother had died during the
year they had been separated and that he had probably
inherited cash as well as property. Mrs. Stein ticked off
one item after another and, without raising her voice
appreciably, would occasionally call out to her daughter:

"Let me know when you want to come down, Meryl."

"I will, Ma. Don't worry," Meryl would answer, obviously able to hear every bitter word Mrs. Stein could
heave at her husband.

According to Irwin Blye, the Stein case is fairly typical
and requires little, if any, work. You check to see if the
man has liens against him. You send a Uniform Commercial Code request to find out what his outstanding debts
might be. You check out his living style for a couple of
days, both midweek and weekend. You check his car
registration. Does he have more than one car? Who is he
seeing? Is he supporting the other woman, as well as his
wife and children? If so, where is he getting the money?

"If you really want to get somebody's net worth," Blye

explains, "it can be done. Especially in divorce stuff. The husband is always telling his wife that things are getting tough. In Mrs. Stein's case he had begun cutting off her credit cards. The bank accounts were changed. Bank-Americard, Master Charge, American Express. Suddenly, after the separation, they can't afford these things.

"What's really going on is that the husband usually has something else going for him when he wants the separation. He has a girl friend. Most of the time she's younger. Most of the time he wants to take her out and live the carefree bachelor life. It costs money. He's supporting a wife and two or three kids. So the money is getting tighter, and when his wife begins asking him for extras, such as money for the kids' clothes at school time or money for her membership at the tennis club, he begins getting sticky about it. Then there are always those little emergencies. The roof sprang a leak. The pipe in the bathroom broke. The separated husband soon feels as though he is being whittled away. Meanwhile, he has to play Fernando Lamas to his new girl friend. This is why separations don't usually work for long. Sooner or later he begins to feel he's getting gypped and that he's better off with a solid settlement and no more. She begins to sense what's coming and if she's smart she'll check in with a lawyer real soon. Also, she should pick her lawyer for his talent in the divorce field. You don't need Clarence Darrow or Cyrus Vance in these cases. What you need is an animal. You need a bomber. The kind of a guy who will get you as much as there is and maybe more. You don't want a nice guy. On top of that, the wives often wind up falling in love for a few weeks with their lawyers. It helps with the tension, and lots of the lawyers don't mind at all.

"But, even after the divorce and the settlement has been reached, that's not necessarily the end," Blye continues. "If the husband is smart or trying to be smart, he'll fix things so that he can go back into court and plead that he's not making as much money as he was at the time of the settlement and ask for a reduction. It's a very common move and one that doesn't get much publicity but keeps lots of private detectives in lamb chops. The reason, typically, is that the man has now married the girl friend and they want their own apartment or house and the guy's new wife is working him over pretty good about how overgenerous he was with his first wife, the bitch, and that he should contest the settlement. Lawyers are never too far behind this kind of bedroom dialogue, and before you know it the guy is petitioning the court. What the hell, the guy and his new wife insist, any reduction they get is more money for them to spend."

Typical of the kind of detective work involved in these cases is a recent one in which Blye represented a woman whose former husband had remarried and wanted to obtain a reduction in his child-support payments because he could no longer afford them.

Blye had been called in by the law firm of Stillman and First. It seemed their client, Lucy Best, was about to lose a substantial part of her child-support payments because her ex-husband, Marvin, had petitioned the court saying that he was now only a salesman for the Sawyer Photographic Company of Syracuse, New York. He claimed he had given up the job on which the amount of the support had been based. Mrs. Best had told Stillman and First that she suspected her ex-husband actually owned the company, but she could not substantiate her claim in court. Enter Blye. He is briefed by both the lawyers and Mrs. Best and shown photographs of Marvin Best. He is given a Dun and Bradstreet report of the Sawyer Photographic Company which lists Robert P. Saunders as president. The report shows that the company did about $400,000 a year in sales and that it did photo enlarging and indexing for retail and corporate accounts.

The very next day, a Friday, Irwin Blye flew to Syracuse, New York. He rented a car and drove to the Sawyer plant at 10 Bay Street. Dun and Bradstreet had reported that the company employed ten people, but Marvin Best was not among the names listed. The Sawyer building was an old, two-story frame converted barn near the Syracuse airport. When Blye walked in, he found five people busily at work. He said that he was a salesman selling industrial supplies and asked if he could speak to the boss.

"It's never as easy as you might hope," Blye says. "In the best of all possible worlds Marvin Best would have come out and said he was the boss. But in this situation a good-looking girl in her mid-twenties came out and said that there wasn't anybody around who could help me. She said Friday wasn't a very good day to see anyone. They were pretty busy. If I called back on Monday, though, she'd be happy to put me in touch with somebody who could help me.

"I asked her for the name of the president or any officer in the company, but all she said was that I should call back on Monday."

Blye then left the building and began taking the license plates of the cars parked outside the Sawyer building. His intent was to get the home addresses and, if they were employees, try contacting them at home about just who did own the company. Blye then drove to the Syracuse Hall of Justice, a large modern building. He went to the Department of Buildings to find out if any special licenses are needed for photographic companies such as Sawyer to operate. If so, he would check to see if Marvin Best had signed any of the required licensing forms. Unfortunately for Blye, there was no special license needed to do what the Sawyer company did.

Blye then went to the County Record room. The Dun and Bradstreet report he had been given by the lawyers was dated October 24, 1975, and stated that Robert Sawyer was the president and that Delia Sawyer was the treasurer. The Syracuse records, however, showed that two weeks after the Dun and Bradstreet report, Mr. and Mrs. Sawyer had the company listed as a Delaware corporation. The secretary of the corporation was listed as a John A. Berman and the attorneys who filed the papers were a Madison Avenue firm from midtown Manhattan.

"I now knew that the company had probably changed hands," Blye says. "So I went to a phone book and looked up a listing for Robert P. Sawyer. If he sold the business, maybe he sold it to Marvin Best and maybe he might be willing to say such a thing. There was a listing for him with an office number listed for the address of the photography plant and a home telephone number listed for 31 High Meadow. I now at least knew the High Meadow Sawyer was the same as the photography Sawyer. That can often be a very tricky thing. You have always got to make certain you have the direct connection. If the telephone book hadn't linked the two Sawyers together, I would have had to call as many Sawyers as I could and ask some vague question about the photography business. One way or the other the identification would have to be made."

Certain that Sawyer was the photography company Sawyer who had recently sold his plant, Blye called him at home. There was no answer. Blye then tried to find the phone listings for a Phillip Heffer listed in Dun and Bradstreet as the company's vice president, and Irving Ritt the company secretary. There was no listing for either man.

Blye then took up the Yellow Pages, and under the heading of Photographic Equipment, Supplies, Wholesale and Manufacturers, he saw that Sawyer was also listed as making small adhesive pricing labels used by many stores. He then looked for the names of other businesses that sold the same kind of labels. Plunking dime after dime into the pay phone Blye would talk with these Sawyer competitors, suggesting that he was a potential customer and was curious about whether or not they had heard that Sawyer had changed hands. None of the salesman and officers with whom Blye spoke knew anything about Sawyer being sold or bought. During these conversations, however, Blye began to pick up the language of the adhesive-label business. When he finally found out what he wanted most to know—the name and amount of an item that Sawyer could not supply—he called Sawyer again.

It was now late afternoon and a woman answered the phone at Sawyer. Blye said he wanted to place a rush order for two million small paste labels of the kind he now knew Sawyer could not supply right away. The woman said that she could not help him, but that she would get someone who could. Within seconds a man was on the phone and identified himself to Irwin Blye as Marvin Best.

"Are you the president?" Blye asked, immediately.

"Well, what exactly is it that you want?" Best answered.

When Blye repeated the order, Best recommended the name of another Syracuse firm that might be able to supply the type and number of labels Blye had requested. Best told Blye that the firm was small, but reliable, and that he had done business with them in the past and had been satisfied.

"Who are you with?" Best asked Blye.

Blye was ready. He had already chosen the name of a large investment firm in the region.

"We're now going into the real estate field and

need the label for various brochures," Blye said.

After hanging up Blye immediately called the company with which Best had said he had done business in the past. Blye used the same label gambit, but this time made it clear that they were getting his business because Marvin Best over at Sawyer suggested he call. Within minutes the owner of the company had let it be known that Marvin Best was an officer in Sawyer and that Best might even be the president of the firm since he seemed to run it.

It was then that Irwin Blye decided to visit the 16 Harwood Circle address in Syracuse that he had been given for Marvin Best by the lawyers. Best lived in a complex of apartments and townhouses in a suburb known as Harwood Estates with his new wife and child. Blye drove to the offices of the renting agent and said that he was a salesman from New York who was relocating in the Syracuse area with his wife and child. The rental agent, a woman, began opening maps of the houses available in the development.

"Just what kind of house are you looking for?" she asked.

"Well," Blye began, "my wife has a friend who visited some people who live in a house here and they had just a beautiful setup. We don't know the people personally, since they are really just friends of friends of ours. Their name was Best, I believe."

The renting agent was delighted.

"Oh, yes," she said, "the Bests live in a townhouse, Model Sixteen."

"Well, I would like the same kind of setup," Blye said. "How many rooms does it have?"

"The Sixteens," the woman began, as Blye took notes, "are two-bedroom townhouses with two floors, a garage, and a basement. They rent from between $280 to $290 a month, plus utilities. You have an option of either gas or electric appliances and the cost averages approximately $60 a month. A $40 deposit is needed to hold an apartment. . . ."

During the rental agent's monologue Blye asked questions about Best, whether she knew where he worked or what he did for a living, but she never responded. Feeling that he had exhausted the source, Blye asked for an application and a copy of the rental brochure that had floor diagrams of the two-bedroom townhouse in which Marvin Best now lived. He thanked the agent and left.

He stopped for a cup of coffee at a luncheonette and waited about thirty minutes. Then he dropped another dime into a pay phone and called the rental company. He got through to one of the company's officers. Blye said that he represented a credit application checking business and that his company could offer a good rate on credit checks if the business could supply them with over one hundred applicants.

"Would you be interested?" Blye asked the rental agent.

"I don't think so," the man said.

"Who does your work now?" Blye asked.

"We use the Greater Syracuse Credit Bureau," the man said, "and we're really very pleased with their work."

"Well, thanks anyway," Blye answered and hung up.

He then called the Greater Syracuse Credit Bureau and, after battling his way through several clerks and minor officials, managed to reach a vice president. Blye said he was the president of a company that was thinking of hiring the Greater Syracuse Credit Bureau to do its credit checking. He said he had been recommended to the Syracuse company by Harwood Estates. He said that Harwood officials had spoken very highly of the Syracuse Credit Bureau while he was checking on a Marvin Best who lived at the estates. Blye said that his firm was finding it less and less profitable to do its own credit-checking and the Harwood people recommended the Syracuse Credit Bureau. The vice president to whom Blye was speaking was pleased with the prospect of a new account. Then Blye asked whether the credit bureau would send along the information on Best and later charge it to Blye's account. The credit bureau vice president said he would do what he could, but he added that he would have to mail the information on Best to Blye's office.

"Fine," said Blye, and gave him the 299 Broadway address.

Blye checked into a motel near the airport. He took a shower and called Herta, on Long Island. She said that she had been having trouble with the carburetor on her Cadillac and he cautioned the children to listen to their mother.

"I'll be home in the morning," he said and hung up.

Then he took his four-year-old Panasonic tape recorder out of his overnight bag, plugged it into the wall, and attached a telephone pickup to the motel phone. Before dialing the telephone he recorded his own voice as he gave the day, the time, and identified himself as a New York State-licensed private investigator.

"I am attempting to reach Robert Sawyer, High Meadow, telephone number 555-8505," Blye said, slowly, enunciating every word very clearly. He dialed the number as he spoke. It was about six o'clock in the evening.

FEMALE VOICE: Hello.
I.B.: Mr. Sawyer, please.
FEMALE: Yes.
I.B.: Mr. Robert Sawyer?
FEMALE: Who is calling?
I.B.: Irwin Blye.
FEMALE: Just a moment please.
I.B.: Thank you.
R.S.: Yeah. Hello.
I.B.: Hello. Mr. Robert Sawyer?
R.S.: Yeah.
I.B.: Hi. I hope you don't mind my calling you on a Friday night. My name is Irwin Blye and I am calling you from New York and we are interested in purchasing a firm such as yours. You've got Sawyer

Photographic, Inc., on Bay Street and I was wondering if you would be interested in negotiating with us.

R.S.: Mr. Blye?

I.B.: Yes.

R.S.: The firm was sold four months ago.

I.B.: Oh, my God.

R.S.: So we are all set.

I.B.: You are kidding.

R.S.: No. And whom do you represent? Are you in the photographic business?

I.B.: Well, we've got pressurized tapes and we put together special brochures. We are in Farmingdale, New York, on Heiser Court. We were looking through the Yellow Pages and we have some clients in the general area and we wanted to acquire a firm up here. I saw your name and you are also listed at your home residence. I thought I'd give you a call and see if there is something that we could do, but—

R.S.: Gee. We are all set, Mr. Blye. We closed the thirteenth of November and we did a good job. So we are all set.

I.B.: The people who purchased it, maybe I could speak to them?

R.S.: Well, they are just starting and they would not see selling for anything.

I.B.: They would not?

R.S.: No. No.

I.B.: Well, maybe then you think they might be interested in handling some of our work?

R.S.: I don't think so.

I.B.: I'd like to give it a shot. We are really desper-

ate for some facilities up here. Something in the
upstate area. It's a problem with us. Could I at least
speak to them. Is there someone I could speak to?

R.S.:   Yeah. You might call 555-6700 on Monday.

I.B.:   Yes.

R.S.:   On Monday.

I.B.:   And who shall I speak to?

R.S.:   Mr. Best. Marvin Best. B-E-S-T.

I.B.:   What does he do, sir?

R.S.:   He is the president of the company.

I.B.:   And he bought it?

R.S.:   Yeah.

I.B.:   I see. Okay. Is he the sole owner or is there
anyone else, sir?

R.S.:   That's right.

I.B.:   He is the sole owner?

R.S.:   Yeah.

I.B.:   Okay.

R.S.:   No. He is not the sole owner, but you have to
talk to him. I forget the details.

I.B.:   But he is the president? Isn't he? Right? Best
is the man to speak to?

R.S.:   He's the man to speak to. He is the president
of the company.

I.B.:   Okay, sir. Then I shall get hold of him, as you
say, on Monday morning.

R.S.:   That's right.

I.B.:   Then I'll give him a call.

FEMALE VOICE: He won't be in on Monday. He'll be
in New York on Monday.

I.B.:   Is he here?

R.S.:   All right. Then why don't you call him Tuesday?
I.B.:   Tuesday. I'll give him a call on Tuesday. Thank you for your courtesy. 'Bye, sir.
R.S.:   'Bye.

The reason Marvin Best would not be at his photo factory in Syracuse on Monday morning was because he would be appearing before a judge in Queens family court pleading with a judge to reduce his support payments. By then, however, Blye had made a transcript of the telephone conversation he had with Robert Sawyer and presented that, along with the rest of the information about Best he had managed to accumulate, to the lawyer representing Best's ex-wife.

The ex-Mrs. Best's lawyers then called Mr. Best's lawyers and informed them of the information they had that proved Marvin Best was far more than a salesman for the Sawyer Photography Company. Best capitulated and withdrew his request for a reduction. Blye never appeared in court. His fee was paid by check by Mrs. Best's attorneys. By the time he got the check Blye was working on several other matrimonials and could hardly remember the details of the case. He barely remembered his trip to Syracuse.

14 **I**t was after six o'clock when Irwin Blye finally got away from Mrs. Stein and the interminable lists of her husband's suspected assets. He slammed the car door shut.

"She's going to be more trouble than she's worth," Blye thought. "She'll never be satisfied. She'll call ten times a day to remind me about the things she's already mentioned dozens of times."

Darkness had set in, and as Blye drove out of Hartsdale, the brightly lit windows of the large and luxurious suburban houses looked like richly decorated department store displays in an illuminated Neiman-Marcus catalogue. Fresh flowers at midwinter, mirrors bouncing and splashing the rooms with gilt, elongated people fixed for an instant with prodigal smiles. Soon, though, it was all gone. Telephone lines that had been hidden under the lawns of the rich suddenly rose out of the earth in great coiled batches, Andy Hardy high schools were replaced by industrial parks, and Irwin Blye was heading toward another world.

The South Bronx, often referred to as Fort Apache by the policemen assigned to the area, is an urban war zone. To live there is to live in a nightmare. The streets are ruled by addicts, drunks, and psychotic adolescents, and for the countless poor forced to live in the area, a simple stroll to the corner store for a quart of milk can be a perilous adventure. When not motivated for profit, the area's shootings, stabbings, and maimings are often the result of minor and imagined slights over parking spaces or jostlings on crowded streets. It was in the South Bronx that the owner of a luncheonette was shot and killed when he failed to provide the apple pie his customer had ordered. It is in the South Bronx where thwarted lovers make a habit of pouring gasoline outside the doors of former girl friends and then lighting fires of vengeance during the night. Since most of these fires are started in rickety slum tenements built before 1900 they account for the deaths of dozens of innocent people every year. It is an area that has been abandoned by everyone lucky enough to escape. The banks long ago ceased giving mortgages and loans to the area's landlords, so the already crumbling buildings have decayed even further. Some landlords turn to the neighborhood arsonist and manage to get some of their money back through insurance scams. When the fire department found the number of tenement fires in the South Bronx was almost ten times that of the other city slums, investigators unearthed a wide-open market in arson. The business was so entrenched in the South Bronx that when six fire marshals tried to arrest one of the neighborhood's best-known torchmen, he was so outraged at their interference with his job that he pulled a gun from beneath his kitchen table and permanently crippled one of the marshals.

"Up here everyone knows when one of the buildings is going to have a fire, because you can see tenants moving their stuff out of the place all day long," Blye says. "The word moves through the street and everybody gets out. It's the ultimate eviction notice."

Tiffany Street was deserted. There were some stores open on Westchester Avenue, about a block away, but once Blye turned off the avenue and began looking for 1050 Tiffany Street everything was still. There is hardly a block in the whole South Bronx that does not have at least one totally gutted building. As Blye drove up to 1050 he noticed that most of the five-story brick tenements on that street had been abandoned. Sheet metal covered most of the windows, but the edges of it had been bent back by junkies who use the buildings to shoot up and to search for saleable items such as copper plumbing, porcelain basins, and toilet bowls. There were

three vacant lots on the block where tenements had
stood, but for one reason or other they had been completely razed and their valuable old brick carted away.
The gaps between buildings were littered with garbage
and the wire fences erected by the city to keep people
away from the rubble-strewn lots had been torn down
and lay twisted in the street.

There was no one visible on Tiffany Street. The inte-
rior of 1050 was almost a refuge. Sounds of music came
from behind closed doors and low-watt bare bulbs gave
some indication that life existed on that grim block. It
was impossible to see who lived in the building as the
brass door that once covered the mailboxes had been
ripped out leaving thirty-five empty mail slots. Some of
the residents had scrawled their last names and apartment numbers on the grimy mustard-colored stucco
wall, but most of the writing was indecipherable.

Mrs. Ann Campbell lived in apartment 4B. Her lawyer,
Phillip Singer, had told her that Irwin Blye would be
stopping by to take her statement about the accident that
had scalded 60 per cent of her body. Singer had told Blye
earlier in the week that Mrs. Campbell had complained
for at least six months that the hot water faucet in the
bathroom was broken. At first she had told the building's
owners every time she paid her rent, and then, when the
owners abandoned the building and it was taken over by
the city, she told various city employees about the ruptured faucet. Singer estimated that the negligence case
was probably worth in excess of $100,000 since Mrs.
Campbell had notified the responsible parties that the

condition existed and, most important, she had been critically injured as a result of the burns, causing permanent scars and impairment even after a two-month stay in a city hospital where she underwent extensive and painful skin-grafting. Singer had heard about Mrs. Campbell from his secretary who employed a cleaning woman who was a friend of one of Mrs. Campbell's daughters. That is the way negligence lawyers get most of their clients.

"Notice is always the key to these kinds of cases," Blye said, shifting his tape recorder and Polaroid camera to his right hand as he made his way carefully up the building's darkened steps while holding onto the banister with his left.

"The woman was scalded by hot water in her apartment. It had been running for six months. She had complained, but nobody bothered to fix the damn thing. There was negligence on the part of the owner. She should be able to get something, especially since her injuries are clearly verifiable from the city hospital's report. She was on the critical list for two months.

"What I have to do is get the superintendent to say that he was aware of the condition of the faucet. If I can get Mrs. Campbell to prove that she complained to both her original landlord and to the city, so much the better. Any notation on a rent check or if the super made a notation of her complaint in his book—fine. If I can get neighbors to say that they saw the leaking faucet and that the water was scalding hot, that will be good, too. Singer wants to show a pattern of negligence on the part of the building's owners and the need for redress on Mrs. Campbell's behalf."

The door to Mrs. Campbell's apartment was open. Light showed in the kitchen where two men and a young woman looked up from the table as Blye entered. No one said anything. Several children who had been playing in the kitchen stopped and looked at Blye with wide, solemn eyes.

"Pardon me," Blye said. I'm looking for Mrs. Ann Campbell. My name is Irwin Blye. Mrs. Campbell's lawyer asked me to see her tonight. He said she is expecting me."

The two men and the young woman said nothing. There were no words of greeting. Finally, the young woman rose and picked up one of the smallest children in her arms. She began walking down a long darkened corridor into the rear of the apartment.

"She's inside," the woman called over her shoulder, without looking at Blye.

He followed the woman into the apartment. The two men seated at the kitchen table scowled amid the litter of empty paper plates and old newspapers and bits of broken plastic on the table before them.

Clothes, electric wiring, a pastel rendering of Jesus, lamps without shades, a junkshop jumble of cheap possessions cluttered every corner of the apartment. And then, in the background, Blye could hear it: the unmistakable roar of water pounding into a tub.

Mrs. Campbell was lying in the middle of a fold-out bed. Three of her toddler grandchildren shared the tumble of blankets and quilts with her. A cluster of bare bulbs hung from a ceiling fixture. There was also an extension cord hanging from the same fixture. It was draped over the top of the bedroom door in a great loop and disappeared into a mass of electrical connections and wires along the apartment's darkened corridor. Mrs. Campbell had difficulty propping herself up when Blye introduced himself. She had been expecting him, she said, but the scars made moving around very difficult. As Blye began asking her about the accident, Mrs. Campbell pulled a huge black handbag from under the quilts and blankets and started rummaging around inside for bits of pencil-scrawled notes relating to her injury. She had rent receipts from the original owners of the building. She had notes from the welfare department about her rent which the city paid.

"How much rent do you pay here?" Blye asked.

"I pay $250 a month for this," Mrs. Campbell said.

"And you complained about the running water?"

"I complained every time I brought the landlord the welfare department rent check," Mrs. Campbell said, "but it didn't do any good."

For at least four years Mrs. Campbell had been paying $250 a month, plus $94 every two months for gas and electricity. The original owner of the building abandoned it in the summer of 1975; in October, New York City took over. On November 24, the day before Thanksgiving, as she had been preparing the holiday for her two daughters, her son, and seven grandchildren who would join her, she tried to turn off the main valve under the bathroom sink. As she knelt she slipped and fell into the tub filled with scalding water.

"Did the police come?" Blye asked.

"No."

"Did anyone call the hospital?"

"Yes."

"Did an ambulance take you to the hospital?"

"No," Mrs. Campbell said, "the ambulance never came. I don't know how long we waited. It was awful. Mr. Jackson, John Jackson, who lives on the block, has a car and took me to Lincoln Hospital."

Blye asked if Mrs. Campbell would mind if he took pictures of her injuries. She did not mind and Blye began snapping Polaroid pictures of Mrs. Campbell's arms and back and neck. The skin was raw and tight and much of it was stretched grotesquely over her body.

Blye then asked if he could photograph the bathroom where the accident took place. The young woman, who was one of Mrs. Campbell's daughters, was instructed to take Blye to the bathroom and show him exactly what had happened.

"Were you here when the accident took place?" Blye asked.

"Yes."

"Were you with your mother when the accident happened?" Blye asked, hoping for corroboration of Mrs. Campbell's claim and an eyewitness to the fact that Mrs. Campbell did not fall into the tub out of drunkeness or madness.

"Yes."

"What's your name?"

"Ruth."

"Ruth what?"

"Ruth Campbell."

"Where do you live?"

"In apartment 3F."

"You mean you live in the same building, but down one flight?"

"Yes."

"What happened the night of the accident?"

"It was about eight o'clock. I was in my mother's apartment and we had finished doing dishes and stuff in the kitchen. My mother left the kitchen and went into the bathroom to turn off the water. The steam and water were on as usual and she wanted to turn the master knob under the bathroom sink. There was water on the floor because the basin was leaking. She went to shut the water off."

"With what?"

"Her arm."

"What arm?"

"Her right arm, to shut the water off. The knob was under the sink, but it wouldn't turn the water off. She tried the knob again and it came off in her hand. Steaming water came shooting out and scalded her. The floor was wet and slippery and I saw her fall into the tub full of scalding water trying to get away from the spray."

Later, Blye retraced Ruth's account of the incident on one of his lined and numbered forms. He had her sign it, including the routine sentence about her having read and understood the above number of lines. Blye also took a statement from Mrs. Campbell and asked whether the building superintendent was anywhere to be seen. Mrs. Campbell immediately dispatched her son, John, one of the men Blye had noticed when he entered the apartment, to find Lester, the superintendent.

While waiting for Lester, Blye took pictures of the bathroom, including pictures of the tub, the broken knob, and the still-running hot water. He took pictures of the layered wallpaper peeling away from the bathroom walls in sodden sheets.

Lester turned out to be a cooperative, though cautious, man. He had been the superintendent in 1050 Tiffany Street for fourteen years and he had lived rent-free in a ground-floor apartment all that time. He was openly solicitous of Mrs. Campbell and Blye sensed that Lester was genuinely sorry that she had been so badly injured. He readily admitted to Irwin Blye that the hot water in Mrs. Campbell's apartment had been pouring out for months and that he was incapable of turning it off. He said the original landlords had promised to send a plumber to fix the faucet, but they never did.

Within minutes Blye had Lester signing a statement that almost guaranteed Mrs. Campbell her claim. It read, in part:

> I was told in the summer by Ann Campbell that the water was steaming hot, running all the time and that she couldn't turn it off. . . .

It had been a long day and Blye had everything that Mrs. Campbell's lawyer would need in presenting her case.

"Even though she was so badly burned," Blye says, "in one way she's a lucky woman. If the city of New York hadn't taken over the building about a month before the accident she probably would never have seen anything like the compensation money she will eventually receive.

"The city is a self-insurer," Blye continues. "So as long as she can convince the comptroller's office, who pays out the money, and the corporation counsel, who challenges her claim in court, Mrs. Campbell will get her money.

"If the building was still privately owned, however, she would have to deal with regular insurance companies and she would eventually get whittled down.

"The regular insurers use two basic techniques," Blye continues. "The first technique is that they try like hell to control the complainant. The minute they hear you've had an accident they're at the house or apartment doing you favors. Need money? Here's a couple of hundred. When things get tight they even send men around to poor claimants with suitcases filled with five- and ten-dollar bills. Most of those poor people have never seen so much money in their lives. The guy takes it out of the suitcase a stack at a time. He's doing them a big favor, you see. He's Puerto Rican, just like them. He's Italian. He's black. He's whatever the claimant happens to be and that's why he's looking out for their interests. It wasn't easy for him to get a suitcase full of money out of the company but he did. If they sign the release it's all theirs. He can leave it right in the middle of the dining room table and walk out the door. It will usually be something like $2,000 to $5,000 in cash on suits that would probably earn the claimant $25,000 to $150,000 if they went through the courts.

"I don't know too many poor people who can resist," Blye says. "Especially after their insurance company buddy says that there are guys in his company who want to fight the case all the way to the Supreme Court, that even if they win it'll take five, ten years, and by then their lawyers will have taken most of the money. These adjustors can be very convincing and most people fall for their line. They will try to provide the claimant with everything. They are all over you like a blanket. Everything from phone calls to chicken soup. It's called 'keeping claimants under control,' and the whole reason behind it is to keep the claimant from getting an outside attorney. They will actually try and pretend they are serving as your attorney, that another lawyer will just take money out of what you will get anyway.

"Depending upon the potential cost of your claim, these insurance companies will go the limit. What they do, of course, is buy you off at a fraction of what you might actually be able to get if you had an outside attorney and followed the case all the way through the courts.

"The other approach," Blye continues, "is the approach taken by most of the mutual insurance companies. These outfits hold out in every single way. No notes about getting well here. They use the theory that by hardnosing each case most claimants will get discouraged and withdraw their suits. It is a conscious corporate policy on the part of many mutuals. They appeal every ruling. They file extraneous motions. They do everything they can to discourage the claim. Mutuals are so tough and hardline that they are often fined by judges for failing to negotiate properly under the state's insurance laws. From this point of view Mrs. Campbell is lucky. She won't be conned and she won't have to fight to the bitter end. With the city she should get her money within a year or two."

15

Within minutes Irwin Blye was on his way out of the South Bronx, driving along the Bruckner Expressway toward the Bronx Whitestone Bridge and his suburban home. It was 10 P.M. The children were asleep. Blye had been to Lake Ronkonkoma in a futile attempt to find Tiny Berels a puncture-proof alibi. He had listened to Mrs. Stein's numbing recitation of her husband's assets. He watched the roaches on Mrs. Campbell's ceiling and had felt the grim reality of her impoverished and unrelievedly brutal life. Telephone calls had riddled the day, lawyers had been called about cases, appointments had been made with witnesses for the next few days, clerks had been cajoled for information during coffee breaks.

At the end of Blye's working day there are no tidy resolutions, no one has been trapped into confessing a crime and no one has been freed. Nothing has been resolved. For Irwin Blye cases are never neatly ordered. The disparate bits and pieces never quite fit. The cases are not organized, the crimes are never codified, the plot is never arranged, and most of the details are missing. He rarely learns what happens to the cases on which he has worked.

On February 24, 1975, almost two months after Blye's inquiries at Lake Ronkonkoma on behalf of Tiny Berels, the South Carolina jury returned its verdict. By then, of course, Blye was chasing after other half-finished cases and tracking down other wrong addresses. He did not even know that the case had gone to trial.

Bob Faucette, Tiny's lawyer and the man who had hired Blye, had taken Irwin's advice and called Mrs. Helen Mann, the bar owner, and Harry Fried, the carnival owner for whom Tiny worked, to appear in court on Tiny's behalf. They were flown south, testified, and were flown home within two days. They did not wait around for the verdict.

Edna Moore, the girl who had accused Tiny of kidnapping her, was in court every day. When she took the stand she repeated her charges and looking directly at Tiny said that he was the man who grabbed her on the street at knifepoint and threw her into the rear seat of the car. She was small, a sweet little girl according to Bob

Faucette, the kind of girl who does not lie. Under cross-examination she did not falter.

At three o'clock in the afternoon on February 24, the jury began its deliberations. They retired at 11 P.M. and were back deliberating at 7:45 the next morning. By 10 A.M. they had reached their verdict.

Judge Robert Chapel called the jurors in and as Tiny Berels stood at the oak courtroom table next to his lawyer and flanked by two beefy court attendants, the jury foreman said they had found him guilty.

Tiny's round face seemed to pale slightly, but otherwise he displayed no visible reaction to the verdict.

Judge Chapel, a tough, no-nonsense judge, said he would sentence Tiny at three o'clock that afternoon.

He did.

By this time, the verdict had registered and Tiny appeared smaller, grayer, less relevant.

"Thirty years," Judge Chapel said. The judge said lots of other things too, but the thirty years was all that anyone in the courtroom heard.

Tiny's attorney, Bob Faucette, was stunned. "It's a tough sentence," he said.

Upon hearing the sentence Tiny's knees buckled just a bit. He began to disappear.

Mrs. Stein continued to call Blye at his office and leave messages on his tape recorder long after she had stopped paying him. Time seemed to have stopped for her and she assumed that everyone involved in her case against her husband brought to it the same bitter passions with which she was awash. Blye had assembled all of the routine information she would need in court. He sat outside her doctor-husband's office in the Bronx and clocked the frequency with which patients were treated. He checked with other doctors to approximate the frequency rate and double-check the fees. From this he was able to estimate how much the doctor actually made as a result of his office practice. Blye estimated through credit references and by following the doctor for a couple of days just about how much money he was spending on himself, his girl friend, his new, emancipated life.

Even with all this, however, Mrs. Stein did not press her separation suit. Despite the fact that her husband kept cutting back on her allowance under the informal arrangement they now had, Mrs. Stein was reluctant to use the information Blye had assembled in order to formalize the separation. She would continue to drift from attorney to attorney, private detective to private detective, accumulating dossiers on her husband that she would never use.

"That's not unusual," Blye later explained. "As long as the separation was informal she still felt that she had him. Once the separation becomes legal, then dependent wives like Mrs. Stein feel they've lost their husbands for good."

As far as Mrs. Campbell was concerned, at least two years of litigation lay ahead. Four months after Irwin Blye drove away from his interview with her, however, the city condemned 1050 Tiffany Street and Mrs. Campbell was evicted. Her attorney, Phil Singer, said that the city marshals had dumped most of her belongings onto the street and she lost much of her furniture. He lost contact with her for a while, because she kept moving from the apartment of one relative or friend to another. He said the first hearing before a city examiner was postponed because the hospital had not yet forwarded the medical reports detailing the extent of her injuries. Singer said, however, that since Mrs. Campbell was a welfare recipient the city would probably expedite her claim, because if she did win any compensatory money as the result of her accident, the Welfare Department would immediately lay claim to all of the money they had extended to her during the period of her destitution.

The endings are never neat. Characters, cases, and resolutions dissipate all over the narrative. There are no final, bittersweet paragraphs on the last page of an Irwin Blye story.

I rode down to the street floor and went out on the steps of City Hall. It was a cool day and very clear. You could see a long way—but not as far as Velma had gone.
Farewell My Lovely by Raymond Chandler

I flipped her pearls out into the water one by one at the floating seagulls.
They made little splashes and the seagulls rose off the water and swooped at the splashes.
Trouble Is My Business by Raymond Chandler

A hundred feet down in the canyon a small coupe was smashed against the side of a huge granite boulder. It was almost upside down, leaning a little.

There were three men down there. They had moved the car enough to lift something out.

Something that had been a man.

The Lady in the Lake by Raymond Chandler

On the way downtown I stopped at a bar and had a couple of double Scotches. They didn't do me any good. All they did was make me think of Silver-Wig, and I never saw her again.

The Big Sleep by Raymond Chandler

He glanced across at Dr. Lagardie who saw nothing and heard nothing, if you could judge by his face.

"I guess somebody lost a dream," the intern said. He bent over and closed her eyes.

Little Sister by Raymond Chandler

At the end of his day Irwin Blye drove home.